Artichoke Heart

*Journey through Loss
to Rediscover the Soul
and Celebrate Living*

Helen Elaine

HARA
PUBLISHING GROUP

Published by
Hara Publishing
P.O. Box 19732
Seattle, WA 98109
(425) 775-7868

Elaine, Helen.
    Artichoke heart: rediscovering the soul
through loss & grief / by Helen Elaine. – 1st ed.
    p. cm.
    ISBN: 1-883697-88-3

    1. Death--Psychological aspects.
    2. Bereavement--Psychological aspects. 3. Grief--
Psychological aspects. 4. Death--Religious
aspects. 5. Bereavement--Religious aspects.
6. Grief--Religious aspects. 7. Soul. I. Title

BF789.D4E43 2000   155.9'37
                 QBI00-500017

Manufactured in the United States
10 9 8 7 6 5 4 3 2

Editor: Vicki McCown
Cover Design: Richard Van Lê
Desktop Publishing: Scott Carnz

Dedications

In memory of and gratitude for the spiritual guidance from my mother, Clara; my sisters, Mary and Pat; my brother-in-law, Phil; and my dear friend, Margaret Cole. Though they reside in the other world, they are always at my side to give me strength and courage to continue my ministry.

In honor of the life and death of my niece, Natosha, and all the abused children around the world.

In celebration of the love and presence of my daughters, Dawn Marie and Robin Ann, who give my life special meaning, bring me great joy, and are constant sources of inspiration.

Acknowledgements

Writing *Artichoke Heart* has created both a sense of loss, as I review my life challenges, and an awakening or rebirth of the creativity of my soul. It has been a challenge as well as an opportunity for personal growth. I want to extend my sincerest appreciation and gratitude to Dr. Lorna Catford, Dr. Eleanor Criswell, Laurie Hope, M.A., Dr. Barry Godolphin, Dr. Frank Siroky, and Dr. Kathy Charmaz, all of Sonoma State University, who have supported me in my research efforts. Special thanks goes to the late Dr. George Jackson for his support and guidance.

Through my experiences at Hospice of Petaluma, this book was born. I am forever grateful to my colleagues and clients for their wisdom, strength, and courage in sharing their journeys with me. Special thanks to my students who have been my teachers.

Recognition and praise go to my family and friends, whose love and support have been my guiding light throughout this process. I honor my daughters, Dawn Marie and Robin Ann, and my son-in-law, Allen; my sisters, Cathy and Jackie; my dear friends, Janice, Kaisa, Judy, and Trish; and special appreciation goes to Mort Robinson. I love each of you and celebrate your presence in my life.

I could not have published *Artichoke Heart* if it were not for the generosity and encouragement of my sister, Marcella; the wisdom and vision of my publisher, Sheryn Hara; and the guidance and expertise of my editor, Victoria McCown. Knowing there are many more to thank, I humbly acknowledge all who have worked diligently to make this book a reality. Much appreciation and love to all of you. May God Bless Each and Everyone of You. Thank You!

Contents

Section One

Exploration and Discovery: The Process

> *Care of the Soul is not solving the puzzle of life; quite the opposite, it is an appreciation of the paradoxical mysteries that blend light and darkness into the grandeur of what human life and culture can be.*
>
> —Thomas Moore

1

Recognizing the Emotional Soul

The Zeitgeist of the 1990s exposes a reality of human pain and suffering that crosses all cultural and socioeconomic boundaries. Children are joining gangs to find a sense of importance and belonging. Adults and children are developing psychological disorders and life-threatening addictions to numb their fears at feeling inadequate and unsafe. Spousal and child abuse are at an all-time high; poverty is a reality; nations still engage in political warfare; insults and violence are the result of prejudice and a need for power and control; and daily we witness a loss of compassion and reverence for human life.

Elected politicians and other social institutions can not make public policy that will arrest the sense of helplessness and hopelessness that blankets our universe. Medical science works diligently to repair the broken and decaying physical body, keeping us alive longer, but we have yet to recognize that without healing the soul of human beingness, our efforts may all be in vain. When I use the term "healing," I do not mean to fix or cure. Healing means to tend or minister to that which is out of balance or harmony from its natural state.[1] A state of naturalness intimates wholeness. Intimacy of wholeness transcends mortality, reaching beyond space and time. It is a matter of sacredness or holiness that joins each of us to the greater realm of cosmic or unity consciousness.

Humanity has always suffered some degree of political unrest, socioeconomic injustice, moral deprivation, and mental and physical dis...ease as it searches for meaning and purpose. This is a complex issue and there is no one answer nor recipe for fixing or curing the ills of humanity. However, I recognize that we each have a responsibility, a duty to contribute to the collective well-being of the human condition. I feel it is my responsibility to share what I have come to understand about the human journey. My hope is that this book will help those who suffer in silence, as well as those who cultivate the mind of human potential, tend to the soul of human emotion and nurture the heart of the human spirit.

At first glance, this book may appear to be a cookbook or gardening guide about artichokes and/or other vegetables. It is not! However, cookbooks are packed full of recipes for nurturing our bodies; and gardening guides explain how to cultivate the soil, providing a rich environment for new growth by recycling natural elements. True to this analogy, *Artichoke Heart* is about nurturing, cultivating, and caring for the human soul.

The artichoke has become a metaphor I use to demonstrate the potential healing nature of the grief process—a journey of rediscovering the soul as we explore the human heart of emotionality. Through the process of removing the prickly thistles and tough leaves of this hardy plant, we arrive at its delicate core, the heart. Similarly, if we remove the layers of emotional pain from the psyche, we get to the heart of our human beingness—the soul which connects us to the Omnipotent Universal Spirit or God. This is what I refer to as the sacred or divine self, which is the core essence of each of us. I have come to know that we can better understand life and all its complexity when we come to terms with the emotional pain that comes from death, loss, and grief. My thesis becomes one of applied psychology, applying what we learn about healing the grief of death to managing the emotions around the anxiety of separation, change, and growth that is inevitable throughout the human life span.

Historically and socially, our culture uses the term "grief" to reference our reaction to the death of a loved one, and it is something most of us are uncomfortable talking about. With the blossoming of the hospice movement and emerging reports of the near-death-experience phenomenon, we are beginning to dialogue about the reality of human physical nonexistence or death. I propose that not only do we need to become more reverent and attentive to the dying process, but it is through understanding this reality that we learn to celebrate life in a healthier and happier convention. We do this by recognizing and honoring all the losses of the human experience and applying the grieving and healing process to a variety of life situations, including: (1) developmental stages and life transitions, (2) divorce and relationship issues, (3) drug and alcohol abuse, (4) physical and mental challenges, (5) terminal illness, and (6) other losses in life.

These human experiences are not linear events in one's life. 5
They are complex, often overlapping, evolutionary processes of change. Change is about learning (attaching), letting go (detaching), and moving forward (transcending) from the known to explore the vast mystery of the unknown. There can be no growth, individual or collective, unless we are willing to accept change. It becomes a matter of human development. It is when we wrestle with the demons of fear and death that we become in tune with the nature of our soul. Paradoxically, by having reverence for our pain and suffering, we begin to celebrate the grace of love and compassion. I feel that we have neglected to study the psychological, physiological, and spiritual manifestations of grief and loss which have deprived us of fully understanding human emotionality and, thus, behavior.

I began formulating this book in my head over six years ago when I was studying psychology as an undergraduate. As I prepared for a career as a marriage, family, and child counselor, I found it difficult to connect the theory I was learning to the ordinary, everyday experiences of my personal life as well as

6

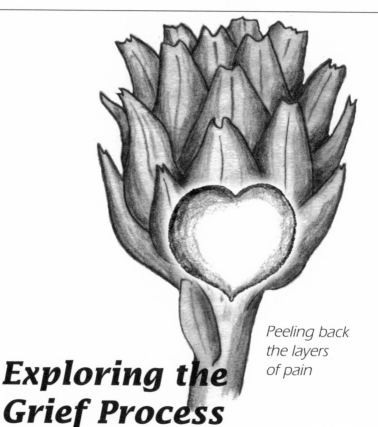

*Peeling back
the layers
of pain*

Exploring the Grief Process

*Healing the Heart
while Rediscovering the Soul*

A mindful approach to understanding and
processing grief as it applies to ALL our losses…

- Death & Dying
- Develpmental Stages & Life Transitions
- Divorce & Relationship Issues
- Physical & Mental Challenges
- Drug & Alcohol Abuse
- Terminal Illness
- Other Losses in Life

TM 1995

those of family and friends. Doubts about academic theory coincided with my training as a hospice bereavement volunteer. My journey with hospice, witnessing and observing the pain and suffering around the issues of terminal illness, death, and grief, provided me with the understanding of what was missing in our attempt to heal the psyche of the living.

I began to realize that healing the psyche was not about curing or fixing the client. I now understand that healing is about sitting with or walking beside another human being as that person moves through his/her grief of life's disillusionment and disappointments, challenges, and sadness. This is a process of the individual "healing thyself" and I am merely a presence of love and compassion, giving the client permission to discover his/her own sacred potential which is a rediscovery of soul. I have come to know that I can best serve humanity by being a spiritual alchemist, teacher/lecturer, writer, and grief counselor.   7

> *The teacher who walks in the shadow of the temple, among his followers, gives not of his wisdom but rather of his faith and his lovingness. If he is indeed wise he does not bid you enter the house of his wisdom, but rather leads you to the threshold of your own mind.* [2]

Reflecting on my personal life experiences and working through the grief of my death-losses gave me a profound awareness that I felt obligated to share with others. Therefore, this book is my contribution to help fill the void between theory and human experience. I believe the field of psychology needs a new paradigm which recognizes and encompasses the interrelatedness of the mind, body, soul, and spirit of our human beingness. Simply stated, my mind-body-soul-spirit theory recognizes that we *must* consider a synthesis of all four of these aspects of the human condition. Whether we are medical, psychological, or spiritual teachers and/or technicians, we *must* care for the "holistic" individual if we are to promote the health of the whole person. My perspective is one of a soul doctor whose ministry is about healing the psyche. It requires that we return to the original Greek concept of psyche, which means "soul" or "the very essence of life."

It is my hope that the Zeitgeist of the twenty-first century will be less remembered for its materialism (which marked the twentieth century) and more remembered for its spirituality. We are an evolving humanity that continues to progress in our creativity of accessing bytes and bits of information that promise the road to the future. As my phenomenological study has pointed out, we seem to have lost something along the way. We have lost sight of the perennial wisdom that has assisted humanity with its challenges since the beginning of time. We have lost touch with the heart and soul of human beingness, both individually and collectively. I find it curious that, as one of the most advanced societies in the world, we continually witness psychological and physical dis...ease as we forge ahead to discover the next frontier for humankind.

I propose that much of our discomfort is a splinteredness of the human psyche. We are not only a culture of strangers; we are strangers to our selves. This estrangement is a sense of unwholeness, driven by our fear of death and resistance to acknowledging the pain and suffering of humanity. We have become patron saints of the "American Dream," the good life, which suggests that the human journey is only about what rights and privileges are inherently bestowed upon us. We look outside ourselves to find happiness, fulfillment, and love. We remain a people divided within our family of humanity while searching for the connectedness we so desperately want and so richly deserve.

I suggest that we look at the end of human life (death, with all its psychological pain and suffering) to discover a new beginning (rebirth) into understanding the mystery of our human beingness. I believe that it is within the paradox of honoring our pain and suffering that we discover *happiness* and *wholeness*, learning to celebrate BOTH life AND death as transformations of energy. Furthermore, I support that we be inclusive and integrate the many schools of western science and the wisdom of eastern philosophy.

When we contemplate or witness death, we begin to question our mortality and explore the meaning of our human beingness. Who am I and what is my purpose on this planet? Mindful reflection of these questions gives us the impetus for spiritual growth and an opportunity to reevaluate those life experiences that teach us that the human journey is about change. Paradoxically, this is an inward journey of self-discovery, as demonstrated by my *artichoke heart*™ metaphor, while being an outward exploration of our relationship to the universal Spirit.

By honestly and reverently looking at the issue of death and dying, we become aware of our angst and anxiety in preparing for this ultimate sense of loss and separation, which I propose as being our transformation from the material world or reunification with the Divine Spirit or God. The human response to the pending death or the loss of a loved one is a sense of grief that manifests in various forms of emotionality. The continuum of emotionality ranges from fear, anger, and denial to acceptance, peace, and love.

Science has different views as to how to classify emotions. I recognize that emotions are psychic energy, meaning energy in motion, and that these emotions have psychological, mental, social, and spiritual properties. Emotions, like dreams, have mystery about them and are part of conscious and unconscious life. There are various studies about the social, physiological, and mental aspects of emotions, but not many from the reference point of the soul. My work pays tribute to all these factors but speaks directly to emotions as being at the heart of the soul, as I feel others have neglected, overlooked, or perhaps been skeptical of this viewpoint.

I looked at emotionality from the reference point of the psyche or soul as it correlates to the anxiety of grief, maintain ing that grief is a necessary and ordinary aspect of being human, not a pathological illness. I recommend that we come to a soulful place of acceptance that the human journey is about both death and life, angst and joy, and that it is a process of *being* or *becoming*. We need to reeducate our society to an understanding that the transformation of death is a natural condition of change and respect the grieving process that inevitably accompanies this reality.

Education and mindful attention to this issue will result in a lesser degree of disenfranchisement to the human psyche as it reacts to other experiences of living. This will help us to handle the anguish, emotionality, and sense of grief that we individually and collectively endure with the ordinary losses and separations that occur throughout the human life span. Paradoxically, this applied psychology of grief teaches us to deal with the more extraordinary loss of death.

10

As we begin to appreciate the mystery of the human experience as a process of being or becoming, we begin to have a reverence for LIFE. Life becomes precious and beautiful. Changing our awareness will benefit all of humanity as we start reacting or behaving from that reference point of heart and soul which entails an awe of life, a respect for life—all of life as being of the Divine cosmic order. We no longer will feel isolated, disconnected, or splintered because we will know we are a part of each other or unity consciousness. We will understand that our human journey in this material/physical realm is about love and compassion, the highest form of energy-in-motion, and come to celebrate the blessings and grace of our beingness as the balance of pain and suffering.

It is necessary that I define some terms and concepts that are basic to understanding this phenomenological study. Due to my holistic paradigm of mind-body-soul-spirit, I integrate William James' concept of the empirical self or "Me" (the self as Known), which includes the material me, the social me, and the spiritual me, with the "I" (the self as Knower), the soul or transcendental ego.³ I refer to this unification as the Holistic Self, with a capital *H* and a capital *S*, and consider it an aggregate that is much, much more than the sum of its parts.⁴

My reference to the physical body is analogous with James' material self, the ego is his social self, and the divine or sacred self is the same as the spiritual self. The divine, sacred, true, or higher self is our connection to unity or pure consciousness, the ultimate potentiality of cosmic energy or what I reverently feel is our connection to God—our Spirit which unites us all as one.

When I refer to the soul, I recognize that it is full of mystery, like dreams, Jungian archetypes, and the unconscious. I agree with theologian and author Thomas Moore that the soul expresses itself in the ordinariness of human existence, music, art, poetry, and emotion. In researching the emotionality of loss and grief, I have borrowed some of Moore's language and concepts of *caring for the soul*⁵, as it most appropriately explains my discovery regarding the pain and suffering of humanity. The terms *tending to, ministering to,* and *cultivating* are analogous and describe a reverence for and attention to a nurturing process which allows for the unfolding of one's self without any predetermined expectations. I am indebted to Moore as a fellow scholar and mentor.

The soul honors the BOTH/AND concept⁶ of human emotionality—a continuum ranging from fear, angst, and sadness to joy, peace, and love. The term *emotionality* embraces the I-Me concept of the self that recognizes that feelings and emotions are characteristic of both the Knower and the Known. Throughout this book I use *beingness* to indicate the noun-form of human beings in an evolutionary state (process) of fulfilling all possibilities (the highest level) of one's fundamental nature. Also, I use the phrase *heal thyself* in a Hippocratic sense, meaning that healing comes from within one's self. As each soul is unique, this becomes an exploration or process of self-discovery into one's true or sacred self. It is to be hoped that the new millennium will see an

11

Holistic Self

1995 Helen Elaine's holistic concept of the self through a mind–body–soul–spirit paradigm.

Unity Consciousness

1895 William James' concept of the self—the Known (Me) includes the material me, the social me, and the spiritual me; and the self as Knower (I), the soul or transcendental ego.

emergence of those of us (soul doctors, if you will) who are integrating spirituality into the study of psychology and arriving at a more holistic paradigm.

This book is divided into three sections. The next chapter discloses my personal experiences of death, loss, and the emotional roller coaster of grief. This information is foundational in understanding why I was submerged in the darkness of despair, and how I began to climb into the light of love and peace. Chapter 3 and Chapter 4 offer insight into my awareness that it is the acceptance and reverence for both life and death and honoring the grief process that reward us with the ability to celebrate the richness of life despite all its challenges. Section Two (Chapters 5-8) is devoted to the applied psychology of loss and grief. It is based on psychological theory, my experiences of academic teaching, the knowledge I have gained from four years as a hospice bereavement volunteer, and extensive research into the manifestations of grief correlating with human emotionality. Section Three (Chapters 9-11) recognizes that the grieving process is in essence an ongoing process of healing. I share some healing techniques and theoretical perspectives which have provided me with the opportunity to heal the splinteredness or imbalance of my psyche. My hope is that you will find some practical strategies to assist in managing your emotional life through all the loss and sense of separation that is inherent within your human experiences. Chapter 12 is a gift to my reader.

13

A sense of loss in regards to self, family,
community, and national spirit has
created an absence of social cohesion.
—Helen Elaine

2

Memories and the Mystery
(My Personal Story)

> There are a thousand and one gates
> leading into the orchard of mystical
> truth. Every human being has his own
> gate. We must never make the mistake of
> wanting to enter the orchard by any gate
> but our own.
>
> —Moshe the Beadle

> Storytelling is an excellent way of caring
> for the soul. It helps us see the themes that
> circle in our lives.
>
> —Thomas Moore

The sixteenth century English poet and dramatist William Shakespeare said, "Everything begins with a story." I believe it is necessary for me to begin with some details of my personal story as it sets the stage for this phenomenological study on the psychology of loss and grief. Our experiences, our perceptions of them, and our memories of both the detailed events and our reactions to these events, are ever so gingerly woven throughout our philosophy and theories. In his book *Makers of Psychology: The Personal Factor*, Harvey Mindess reminds us of

Nietzsche's words "that each one of their philosophies is the confession of its author."[1] It is impossible to separate personal experience from academic learning. With an integration of both experience and knowledge, a wisdom begins to emerge. I offer the following disclosure as foundation for why and how I have come to believe in my message of learning to celebrate life through understanding death, loss, and grief.

Act One: The Long Night of Childhood

My drama begins fifty-two years ago in a small farming community in Iowa. Born into a poor, Irish, Roman Catholic family, I was the sixth of nine children, eight girls and one boy. My earliest memory (until age regression therapy a few years ago) was of falling out of a gate swing and splitting my head open on the rough, jagged edges of the sidewalk. I was four years old. My father would not allow my mother to take me to town for medical treatment although it was only six miles away, so she sopped up the blood with a towel, instructed me to hold ice on it, set me in an armchair and told me not to go to sleep as I might become unconscious. The physical pain was unbearable, but I was afraid to cry. Every twenty minutes or so she would come check on me, gently shaking me and reminding me not to fall asleep.

My second childhood memory was later that day when my mother put my baby sister in my arms and said, "Hold her tight and don't drop her." I loved holding my baby sister but was afraid that I would do something wrong. The following year, Mom put another baby into my arms and by the time I was ten, the ninth child was born. My mother told me to protect these babies with my life. I loved them as if they were my own. These adolescent years became a terrifying nightmare as my father evolved into a violent, raging alcoholic. I can remember hundreds of nights rocking my youngest sister, praying on rosary

15

beads while Dad physically abused Mom. My older siblings tried to stop him, but they couldn't—we were just children.

Due to this traumatic environment I developed asthma and spent many nights fighting for what I thought was my last breath. Again, my father would not allow treatment of this illness as he said that the doctors didn't know anything and they just wanted his hard-earned money. I have not had an asthma attack since I was fifteen, when I began living with older, married siblings. This is proof to me of the mind-body connection and psychosomatic illnesses. My father raged sometimes all night and we children never got any sleep. We used to hide out in the closets, barn, root cellar, anywhere so we wouldn't become one of his victims.

After each war upon my mother, there would be a day of silence—no one dared discuss what had happened. I learned very early to bury my feelings! I wanted to cry and scream at him when I saw my mother black and blue for days afterwards. I also learned to repress my anger and tears. I remember many times when my older sisters and I would dump all the hard liquor down the drain and hide all the butcher knives. We all lived in constant fear that one day he would kill our mother and then come after us. My father would drink close to a fifth of whiskey and a case of beer a day, day after day, week after week, and month after month.

I remember one summer day when I was eleven. My mother had gone to a 4-H meeting and taken the younger children with her. Two of my older sisters and I were told by Dad to go weed and hoe the garden. But it had rained the night before and Mom had instructed us not to set foot into her garden, even if Dad told us to, as we would pack the soil. So we decided to run from him. He got on the tractor, shotgun in hand, and chased us for miles. We were barefoot and the gravel roads tore our poor little feet to shreds. He fired a few shots occasionally, missing us thank God, and we hid in a roadside ditch and waited for our mother to return. There are many more terrifying memories, some good ones, and lots of blank spaces in my childhood.

Our family religion proposed a dichotomy that took forty years to reconcile. As a child I prayed to God to turn my nightmare existence into peace and happiness. I took on a huge sense of guilt as my father's drinking and violence got worse. If God didn't answer my prayers, then I reasoned that I must be bad. I was doing something awful. I would surely go to hell. I remember once when my mother went to confide in the parish priest (they were the counselors in those days) about how Dad beat her. She was told to go home and be a better wife and mother and then my father would not get so angry at her. The patriarchy and hierarchy of our church, which should have comforted and counseled my mother, sent her back for more punishment. I was so confused. I loved God, praised and worshiped Him, but couldn't understand why we had to live like this. I was supposed to love and honor my father; it was a sin to hate. But, how can you love and respect someone who is such a madman?

As children, all we could do was pray and join together to try and protect ourselves and our mother. When we got older we would call neighbors and the county sheriff to stop him. Occasionally, they would come to the farm, but Dad would talk to them about cattle prices and crops and they would leave thinking we children were crazy. No one wanted to get involved. The sheriff said that he couldn't do anything until my father killed someone. Well, twenty-five years ago, he did kill our mother and the county and state authorities did nothing.

I was twenty-six years old and living in California when I got the call that the nightmare was over. Mom was dead. I was relieved as he could no longer hurt her. Mom, at the young age of fifty-seven, was going to live with Jesus now and finally be at peace. Of course, we children knew it was due to all those beatings; she died of a cerebral hemorrhage. Again there was a silence. No one discussed it until my father died, sixteen years later. It was too painful for any of us to bear. I could not understand this delusion. It did not make any sense. I kept asking WHY? This was the beginning of yet another spiral into my abyss of pain and suffering.

In his heartfelt description of life in the concentration camps of Nazi Germany, recorded in his 1986 Nobel Peace Prize book, *Night*, Elie Wiesel states:

> *Never shall I forget that night, the first night in camp, which has turned my life into one long night...never shall I forget those moments which murdered my God and my soul and turned my dreams to dust. Never shall I forget these things, even if I am condemned to live as long as God Himself. Never.* [2]

18 I agree with Wiesel's perception; we should never forget. Our Creator has given us the mental capacity to remember. This is not to prolong our suffering; it is to alleviate it. Our memory is a wonderful gift that allows us to go forward in a different light so that we can heal. Forgive maybe; forget never. If we forget these acts of power and violence, then cruelty and injustices will continue to plague humankind. Rumi, an ancient Sufi poet and mystic, said, "I use memory...I don't let memory use me." [3] We must all learn to use our memories wisely in an act of healing the spirit of humankind. We must examine our lives and experiences so we can understand the self and reevaluate meaning and go forward. I know now that my ongoing relationship with God is what gives me hope, courage, and strength to face the adversities of life.

Act Two: Developing the False Self

I was happy and smiling the day I married my high school sweetheart. Being twenty-two days from my nineteenth birthday, I looked at life as an adventure. I thought I could leave all the pain of my childhood in Iowa as my new husband and I moved to California. We had a wonderful life together except for our disagreements about drinking alcohol and going to church as a family. I had been to Mass every Sunday of my life, and even though my husband had joined Catholicism, he would not go to church with me. This created a huge void in my life. He never told me that I couldn't go alone, but he would plan weekend outings that did not include time for church. I felt guilty if I didn't do things with him on weekends as we didn't see each other much during the week due to our jobs. Eventually, I quit going to church.

After three years of marriage, our first daughter was born. My husband and I both believed it was important that I stay home with our children even though we were of the generation where women were going outside the home to work. But when my husband returned to college, it became necessary for me to work. We put our daughter in nursery school when she was two and a half years old. It was so hard to leave my little baby with strangers; this created a sense of loss and guilt.

God blessed us with our second daughter five and a half years later. She was born with a condition they called a soft palate and had surgery at nineteen months of age. Fortunately, her prognosis was good. Once again I found myself going back to work. I had challenges with both babies. I felt great during my pregnancies; but my first baby cried and fussed until she was eighteen months old, never sleeping through the night, and my second daughter was hard to feed due to her physical impairment. However, I realized how lucky we were to have two beautiful, healthy daughters. I was grateful and began to realize that God had not forsaken me.

The first fifteen years of our twenty-five-year marriage were happy ones. Somewhere during this time, I began to drink so that I would fit in when socializing with our friends. And when

I began drinking, my husband and I no longer argued about his drinking. It seemed to make our lives more joyful and peaceful.

When I tried to drink hard liquor or wine I would get hives and heart palpitations. Now I know this as a sign of genetic alcoholism; I am allergic to alcohol. Our friends made fun of me, kidding me that I wasn't a good drinker. Finally, I discovered that my body could handle beer, so that became my drug of choice. It seemed that I could have a few beers, fit in with the adults, care for my two children, husband, and home, hold down a full-time job, and occasionally go to night school.

Due to the fear, heavy sense of responsibility, and state of hyperalertness that I was raised in, I became overly vigilant about taking care of everyone and everything at the cost of burying my true self in the darkness of the subconscious. However, when we do this we lose sight of our spirit (our sacred self), creating a hole in our soul which swallows up the essence of who we really are and crushes any chance of becoming whom we have the potential to become.

20

As the false self continued to emerge, I buried my feelings, thoughts, and desires, since it seemed every time I tried to express them I was accused of nagging and bitching. I remember feeling that I was supposed to "get on" with life and quit dwelling on my past. So I tried to move on. I developed a serious case of ulcers by the time I was twenty-nine and my sinusitis and allergies got worse. Also, I had been plagued with menstrual problems since I was seventeen and the symptoms increased. By the time I was thirty-two I had cystic ovaries, migraine headaches, severe endometriosis, dangerous fluctuating blood pressure, the PMS crazies, and symptoms of early menopause.

For five years I was treated by male doctors who told me to relax and prescribed painkillers for the cramps, hormones for the chemical imbalances, and Valium for my unsettled nerves. They advised me to see a psychiatrist. Well I did! This was perhaps the most humiliating and degrading experience of my life. As I walked into his office, before I could sit down, and even before he introduced himself, this psychiatrist screamed at me, "You are the daughter of an alcoholic and I can fix you." I burst into tears, allowed him to abuse me verbally and emotionally for forty-five minutes, and finally walked out, never to see this man again.

My husband, my children, and I were convinced that I was an alcoholic like my father. Thank God I never resorted to being abusive or violent. Overdrinking became a monthly event and I would call my sisters, crying about how unhappy I was. The mood swings caused by early menopause and alcohol did not mix. During these episodes I would get very melancholy and try to express my thoughts and feelings to my husband. He was the silent type and did not want to discuss matters of the heart. We would get into an argument and I would end up ranting and raving, trying to release the angst of my soul. I felt so confused and desperate. No one seemed to understand what I was telling them—that I was depressed, sad, lonely, tired, scared, and feeling unloved—afraid to live and afraid to die.

Finally, I found a female general practitioner who threw all my medications in the garbage can and started over. She recommended that I see a licensed social worker and I did for a few months until my husband got so angry about the bills that I had to quit. The saving grace of my work with this therapist was that he suggested that I go to Alcoholics Anonymous. By this time I was drinking daily and my life was out of control. I have never been so sad, scared, depressed, and confused. A sense of helplessness and hopelessness invaded my personality and behavior. My heart literally ached as I slipped into the abyss of darkness.

During my first AA meeting, I was frightened and could not relate to anyone's story. After the meeting, over coffee and cigarettes, I confided in a kind woman who recognized my discomfort. She said. "I don't think you belong here; you belong in ACOA or ALANON." What was she talking about? I had never heard of these things. I realized that not only did I not fit in

21

with my husband and his social circle, but I was such a loser that AA didn't want me either. I was so LOST.

Act Three: Saving Grace of Allies

My female physician explained these new terms to me and encouraged me to go to a meeting of Adult Children Of Alcoholics. Also, she and I were convinced that, after trying all kinds of hormone replacement therapy, I needed a complete hysterectomy. I had this much-needed surgery at the age of thirty-seven at which time I developed hypoglycemia. Except for the forty-pound weight gain, my hysterectomy was a blessing. I began to feel sane again and thrilled to get rid of the physical pain which I had been enduring three weeks out of every month. The migraines, high blood pressure, and other symptoms disappeared.

When my seventeen-year-old daughter sat at the bottom of her father's and my bed two Saturday nights in a row, crying and telling us that she and her sister were concerned that Daddy and I were becoming alcoholics, I dumped my last can of beer down the drain. This young woman had so much love and courage, mixed with fear and sadness in her heart, that I knew this was the end of the line for me. I guess this is what alcoholics refer to as hitting bottom. Well, I hit it and hit it hard. I was so ashamed! The sad thing was her father's denial. He told her to mind her own business.

I sat in ACOA and ALANON meetings every Friday night for two years and listened—listened with my heart as others wrestled with the demons in their soul. Finally, after practicing silence for all those months, I spoke; and I have not quit speaking out since. I had finally found a home—a place where people understood what I felt and thought. They listened with love, compassion, and, most important, without judgement. In his book *Further Along The Road Less Traveled*, the noted psychiatrist and lecturer M. Scott Peck shares the story of C.G.Jung's indirect involvement with Bill W. and the beginning of AA:

> *... While there were not many people that he, Jung, could talk to about such things, it had occurred to him that it was perhaps no accident that we traditionally referred to alcoholic drinks as spirits, and that perhaps alcoholics were people who had a greater thirst for the spirit than others, and that perhaps alcoholism was a spiritual disorder, or better yet, a spiritual condition.*[4]

I agree with Jung's observation as I know the spiritual deprivation of this family disease. Though my family of origin practiced devout Catholicism, we were living in fear of my father's drinking. This constant state of fear separated me from the Spirit of God and created a lost soul. I literally shudder and feel sick to my stomach as I recall that desperate feeling. John Bradshaw, author of *The Family* and *Creating Love*, recognizes alcoholism as a "hole in the soul" of each family member, as it can destroy everyone that the alcoholic is close to.[5] During my recovery, Bradshaw's wisdom became a lifeline for me. I attended workshops, lectures, and watched his PBS specials on family dynamics repeatedly for about five years.

As so often happens, we marry the image of our fathers. Both the men that I was supposed to be able to trust with my heart were alcoholics. I have learned that their pain is so great that there is no entrance into the sanctuary of their soul. They are incapable of giving and receiving love. There is no love without intimacy and no intimacy without clarity of spirit, which abuse of alcohol denies.

My raging was over. I was learning that I was wasting too much energy trying to get my husband to understand me; the real challenge was for me to begin to understand myself. Who was I? As I began living the ALANON philosophy and changing my behaviors, the emotional distance between my husband and myself widened.

23

I was still in my false self, a defensive mode, but sobriety gave me clarity of mind to begin a journey of self-discovery and well-beingness that I am still traveling today. I want it clearly understood that I do not blame or hold anyone responsible for my abusive drinking. No one forces an alcoholic to drink; we do it to ourselves. I unconsciously used alcohol as an emotional pain-killer. As the silence between my husband and me grew louder, I feared losing my marriage. Thoughts of divorce went through my mind. But I could never get a divorce; it was out of the question due to my religious obligations.

One day I received a message from a Higher Power to study psychology. I guess my intellect needed to make sense of my reality and the world surrounding me. When, at the age of forty-one, I made the announcement that I would begin community college in the fall, my husband talked supportively but was not thrilled that I was going into the field of psychology. My children were excited for me and proud that their mommy was going to college.

Act Four: A Self-Actualizing Process

During the second semester of my academic career, I was presented with yet another challenge—the cathartic event of an automobile accident in which I broke three cervical vertebrae (C-4, C-5 & C-6). I remember thinking that, as the car left Highway 101 and became airborne, I would surely die when my vehicle came to rest back upon the earth. After counting three air-rolls, I felt a stillness and silence which cannot be described in words. I did not know where I was, only that the car had stopped its flight. Immediately, I was talking to God and praying that He would take care of my children. After reciting a heartfelt Act of Contrition, as my sins passed through my mind, I realized that I may not be dying. At this moment, I also recalled all my blessings in life. Survivors of near-death experiences refer to this as a "life review."

24

I told God that I was ready to join Him if He thought it was my time. Intuitively, I believed He decided such things.

After what must have been only a few minutes, a man was asking me if I was conscious. This intrusion broke the silence and beauty of my altered state of consciousness and brought with it the greatest physical pain I have ever known. I told him that my neck was broken. He kept asking me my name, address, the date and year, and other statistical questions, making sure that I remained conscious. He had already called the paramedics. I tried to move, thinking that I could crawl out the broken windshield. I pulled out my right arm and unlatched the seat belt only to realize that I was upside-down and pinned in. I was not going anywhere! I discovered later that I was crushed into a very limited space; no wonder I lost over an inch of height and have a severely compressed spine.

The physical pain was unbearable. I remember praying that I would pass out so I couldn't feel the pain. I remained conscious through the entire event and knew that it was important that I remember everything. I continued to repeat the Serenity Prayer for over an hour while they rescued me with the jaws of life. As I lay strapped to a board in the right lane of the freeway, I became aware that I was exposed to the world in my bra and panties. It had been necessary to cut my clothes off to get me out. As I felt the rain on my body, I was so grateful that my daughter had not commuted with me that day and so very thankful just to BE ALIVE.

After two surgeries and twenty-two days in the hospital, I went home to recuperate. I had three bone grafts (fusions) with a permanent surgical clamp attached to C-5 and C-6 to prevent me from becoming a quadriplegic. Two of my sisters and my mother-in-law came from Iowa to care for me for a few weeks while my husband arranged for a permanent housekeeper and caregiver. My daughters (then fourteen & nineteen years of age) and their neighborhood girlfriend were the angels who cared

25

for me the most. I was in a halo for four months and a hospital bed for six. My husband's drinking got worse as he couldn't deal with me being unable to function as I always had. As I recall, he never once told me that he was sorry that I was injured or that he loved me. He angrily kept referring to the fact that I had wrecked his car and that this whole ordeal was costing him too much money. This attitude was so familiar as I recalled my father's lack of concern and compassion when I was a child. I can not judge or analyze my husband's thoughts and feelings, as he chose self-medicating with alcohol instead of sharing what real effect this had on him. I am sure his fears were as real as mine even if he wasn't conscious of them. We grew further and further apart.

After learning to walk alone again, I began driving myself to physical therapy. We don't realize how much we automatically use our neck and upper body while driving. It is a task that still causes me pain today, ten years later. I remember that when I helped do the Christmas dinner dishes that year, I could see my husband and the girls thought Mom was okay and could resume her regular duties. This was not the case. Yes, I can do the dishes—in fact I enjoy doing them—but I shouldn't vacuum and do other housework as it requires movement that brings on intense pain. But we were trying to put life back into its normal routine, which meant that I was to take care of everyone and everything once again. Needless to say, this was a false reality; I would never be the same again.

My sense of hopelessness and helplessness grew more desolate, so I went back into therapy. After several visits, the therapist requested that my husband join our sessions. He felt my problems were marital. My husband went for five sessions, kept his arms and legs crossed and jaw set through the entire time, and only opened his mouth twice. The first time was day one when he said that he would not quit drinking for anyone. The fifth session he echoed the same statement and said he was not coming back to therapy as it was "bullshit." On the way home he said, "Go get your divorce." I was devastated! I thought we were still trying to hold our marriage together, but he wouldn't or couldn't, and that was that.

A year before my auto accident, we had gone to a marriage encounter weekend and felt that we could still walk life's path together. Now, this was no longer a reality. I was confused as my husband and I had promised each other that we would <u>never</u> divorce, that whatever problems arose in our marriage, we would work through them together. Also, my wedding vows were very important to me, to break them seemed sacrilegious. Once again I felt like a failure and a sinner. My husband and I separated for a year, and divorced the following summer, a few weeks before our twenty-fifth wedding anniversary. I have learned to never say *never*.

Act Five: An Awakening— Opportunities and Choices

After two years of physical therapy, I knew I must come to terms with the fact that I was permanently disabled. My accident was both a blessing and a curse. During this time, I continued psychotherapy and began to face the demons of my soul: (1) the effects of childhood events on my adult behavior and personality; (2) understanding my father's and husband's disease of alcoholism; and, (3) taking responsibility for my emotional immaturity and drinking habits.

It was through autohypnosis and age-regression therapy that I tried to heal my emotional scars. This is extremely hard work, but well worth the struggle. During these sessions I finally acknowledged the importance of my sexual victimization some twenty years earlier. It is still hard to talk about; but, the fact is that I was raped by my brother-in-law. Far beyond the abuse that is inherent in such an ordeal was my husband's reaction, or I should say lack of reaction, to my victimization. He assumed a greater victim role as I would not allow him to kill my sister's husband for his revenge. My thoughts were to protect my sister and her three small children, and I did not want my husband to go to prison for murder. I buried my emotional pain deep inside my soul, only to have it resurface some twenty years later.

I cannot fully describe the healing process that accompanies a forty-year reality of living in a state of helplessness and hopelessness. I cannot put a time frame on my physical, emotional, psychological, and spiritual healing. This process transcends the concept of time and becomes a matter of evolving consciousness, personal reflection, and mindful practices. I know that everything comes full circle and that it is with true *grace and grit*,[6] that we not only survive but we go forward in a new light.

This new light or consciousness transcends time-bound awareness and offers each of us an opportunity for growth and self-actualization of the most sacred dimension. More important, it causes a profound, collective ripple effect touching all of Creation in ways that the individual will never fully comprehend. I can honestly report to you that my sense of helplessness and hopelessness has been replaced with joy, love, light, hope, and peace.

The grit it took to go through the knowledge-gaining rigors of academia, the learning to cope with my disability, the soul-searching struggles of psychotherapy, the discipline of living the twelve-step philosophy, and the opening up to a somatic (mind-body) awareness have all served to mend my personhood and enrich my life. However, I was still missing a piece to the mystery of healing. In my third year of college I participated in a community involvement class that led me to the local hospice. It was when I began dealing with matters of death, loss, and grief that I finally found my saving grace.

I completed the bereavement volunteer training course and began assisting family members who had recently lost a loved one. I did this work for over four years, serving as a one-to-one counselor and group facilitator. Actually, it is not work, but a privilege and an honor to witness the transformation that takes place as each bereaved individual finds new meaning to life and goes forward in the spirit of what I call *community consciousness*.™

What had been missing in all my recovery was learning how to honestly deal with emotions. Experts tell us to feel our feelings but no one explains how this is done. Not one of the professionals whom I saw, nor any of the group work which I did, nor all the psychology courses which I mastered ever mentioned the emotionality around loss or grief. What was missing was a witness to my pain and suffering. I have come to realize that we all need someone who will walk with us as we find our own way towards the light that awaits us. We do not need someone to try and cure or fix us, but someone who cares enough about another human being to accompany us on our journey of healing, which only we can do.

When human beings learn to step outside the ego-self, they have the freedom to take on the pain of those who suffer. This creates a welcomed respite for the sufferer, a fresh breath; then the person in grief can reach down inside their heart and soul and discover the Divine Spirit that gives them the strength and courage to go forward. This is love, mature love that requires putting someone else first.

My story is not that different from millions of others. For example, throughout mythology runs a familiar thread about the search for the divine self and the meaning of life. It is not so much about what individual experiences we endure, but more about how we think, feel, perceive and remember the events, react to them and choose to carry them forward with us either as a prison or as a key to our freedom. By choosing to explore the drama of my childhood, witnessing the development of my false self, and the saving grace of allies, I have discovered an awakening of my divine self that helps me to walk forward in a consciousness of actualizing all my human potential.

Perhaps, as Thomas Moore suggests, if we pay more attention to caring for the human soul and nurturing the human heart, we will discover what we need to bring humanity to a peaceful place of sacred homeostasis—a consciousness of honor and reverence for the gift of life which has been bestowed upon all by our Creator.[7]

> *The unexamined life is not worth living.*
> —Plato

> *The way we respond to pain is the way*
> *we respond to life.*
> —Stephen Levine

3

The Paradox of Life and Death

We are creatures in two worlds—the world beyond this one, and this one.
                                          —*Jacob Needleman*

And if one is not able to die; is he really able to live?
                                          —*Paul Tillich*

In Chapter Two, my personal story illuminates the pain and suffering of the human experience. It is because of these experiences and my dedication to contribute to the healing of others that I have arrived at this phenomenological study of loss and grief as it correlates to the separation and anxiety that are inexorably present throughout the lives of each of us.

Human pain and suffering comes in two forms, psychological and physical, each having many interrelated components. Pain is a signal that something is wrong. Psychological pain is a reality of grieving that which is lost. It is a separation or splintering of the soul. The psyche is out of balance. Before we can begin to understand the manifestations of grief and its correlation to human behavior, it is imperative that we have a discussion about death—the ultimate sense of loss.

The Mystery

Like much of ancient mythology, my perspective assumes that we come into life—the human, physical state of matter—from a descent of Spirit, and then as we die, we ascend or return to the Spirit becoming one with unity consciousness. This is both a natural and sacred process. The Eternal Spirit is that which withstands and encompasses all time and space, all energy and matter, all information and potentiality, also referred to as the Omnipotent Consciousness or God.

The human experience is a collective consciousness, an awareness of "being in process" in a material world of matter on the planet Earth. In existential terms, individual existence is Dasein (*sein* means "being" and *da* means "there" or "being there"), recognizing that we have descended into a time-bound state of human beingness and therefore become responsible for our own existence while visiting this realm of self-awareness. This responsibility is about the *potentia* or source of potential that is in constant motion or process. Simply put, it is about becoming who we are meant to be.

As the spirit joins the forces of nature, a being emerges that has characteristics of both the sacred and the profane. This convergence of spirit with the natural or material realm manifests itself as a soul traveling in the vehicle of the highest evolution of matter—known as the human being or being human. I realize I am suggesting that we wed the history of evolution with the story of Creation, as I feel that somewhere within this synthesis we will discover the meaning of human existence. In his Pulitzer Prize winning book, *The Denial of Death*, Ernest Becker discusses such a marriage of these two phenomena. As he explores Kierkegaardian philosophy, he states:

> *The fall into self-consciousness, the emergence from comfortable ignorance in nature, had one great penalty for man:*

32

*it gave him dread, or anxiety. One does not find dread in
the beast, says Kierkegaard, "precisely for the reason that
by nature the beast is not qualified by spirit." For "spirit"
read "self" or symbolic inner identity. The beast has none.
It is ignorant, says Kierkegaard, therefore innocent; but
man is a "synthesis of the soulish and bodily" and so expe-
riences anxiety. Again, for "soulish" we must read "self-
conscious."[1]*

In this quote from Kierkegaard, we hear the terms "spirit" and
"self" or inner identity as having analogous meaning. This refer-
ences the spirit in all of us: the Atman-Brahman concept—the
Buddha within, the Christ within each higher form of life which
is related to pure consciousness or God. The "soulish" referenced
by Kierkegaard describes the human energy's gateway to this
sacred realm of Eternity.

I believe, as do the Native Americans, that all of life (mineral,
plant, and animal) has spirit as part of its constitution. What
makes the human condition different is that we have a higher
evolving consciousness; we are aware of, or should be aware of,
our union of opposites—self-consciousness and physical body.
With consciousness, we recognize that we are part of the Di-
vine that exists forever even though our physical body is sub-
ject to decay and death.

As do many philosophers and mystics, I acknowledge that
this paradox is what causes human angst, dread, or anxiety. The
paradox of life and death—BOTH self AND not self, BOTH
being AND not being—is what we must learn to hold in sacred
reverence. I propose to you that the fear of physical death is at
the core of most psychological dis...ease or imbalance. And, it
may well be at the root of many physical ailments.

The mythological story of Adam and Eve in the Garden of
Eden is perhaps the most referenced analogy of understanding
this mystery. With the fall of Adam and Eve from the grace of

God came the awareness of both good and evil, right and wrong, life and death. Humans were no longer to be in a state of peace and harmony in union with God, but in a state of flux and change, responsibility and choice, pain and suffering with joy and ecstasy.

I teach my students and clients that we must embrace the BOTH/AND concept that recognizes the human experience as a union of opposites. The human experience is about BOTH life and death, BOTH angst and euphoria, BOTH sadness and joy. If we can understand this concept and recognize that we are still connected to unity consciousness which makes us all the same, then we begin to honor ourselves and each other as "sacred beings" in evolution or process of becoming. Death is merely the transformation and resurrection from our physical state of matter to the highest state of unity consciousness. This is an exploration of discovering one's own meaning into the mystery of life and death.

As we have evolved physically, we have lost our ontological sense of being in the world. The physical and materialistic have replaced our spirituality and sense of unity, both of which are necessary for us to remain in a state of balance and harmony. With this comes a loss of meaning and purpose. We have lost our relationship to our soul, and the ego-self has emerged as our most significant reference point.

Demystification of the Ego

If we are to understand the polarities of the soul, we must take a look at the human ego. Sigmund Freud, the famous founder of the school of psychoanalysis, gave us the term *ego* some one hundred years ago to refer to that part of the human personality that deals with the objective world. Freud's *id* knows only the subjective reality of the mind (which controls the total organism) and is only interested in whether an experience is painful or pleasurable. He refers to this primary process as the "Pleasure Principle." While the motivation for our behaviors may come from the id or subjective realm, our ego, which must deal with the objective environment, functions to decide or make choices as to which and how these primary instincts will be satisfied. Freud refers to this secondary process as the "Reality Principle."[2]

To balance the influence of the pleasure-seeking id on the ego is the *super-ego*, which develops as an individual becomes socialized to the values, norms, and ideas of a society. As for the super-ego, "...its main concern is to decide whether something is right or wrong so that it can act in accordance with the agents of society."[3]

Freud recognized that the original source of human energy resides in the id. I would like to extend Freud's definition of this original source and offer it as coming from and being of the SOUL. I think it is a much larger concept than mere biological and physiological drives, instincts, and needs. It has a spiritual component which is present prior to the development of the id, ego, and super-ego. Many neo-Freudians recognize that Freud was aware that his triad of id, ego, and super-ego were forms of energy that were intrinsically interrelated.

With Freud's metaphor of the mind as an iceberg, 10 percent exposed as the conscious and 90 percent submerged as the unconscious, he suggests that there is a world unknown to humans which houses "...the urges, the passions, the repressed ideas and feelings, a great underworld of vital unforeseen forces that exercise an impervious control over the conscious thought and deeds of individuals."[4] I believe—as did Carl Jung when he extended Freud's concept of the unconscious—that the unconscious is collective and is our connection to the other world which is of the Divine Spirit or unity consciousness. As Carl Jung is one of my favorite theorists, I would like to quote a lengthy message from an essay of his in Herman Feifel's edited book, *The Meaning of Death*.

35

At all events, experience shows that religions are in no sense conscious constructions but arise from the natural life of the unconscious psyche and somehow give adequate expression to it. This explains their universal distribution and their enormous influence on humanity throughout a history which would be incomprehensible if religious symbols were not at the very least truths of man's psychological nature.... Hence it would seem to be more in accord with the collective psyche of humanity to regard death as the fulfillment of life's meaning and as its goal in the truest sense, instead of mere meaningless cessation. Anyone who cherishes a rationalistic opinion on this score has isolated himself psychologically and stands opposed to his own basic human nature. This last sentence contains the fundamental truth about all neurosis, for nervous disorders consist primarily in an alienation from one's instincts, a splitting off of consciousness from certain basic facts of the psyche. Hence rationalistic opinions come unexpectedly close to neurotic symptoms. Like these, they consist of distorted thinking which takes the place of psychologically correct thinking. The latter kind of thinking always retains its connection with the heart, with the depths of the psyche, the taproot. For enlightenment or no enlightenment, consciousness or no consciousness, nature prepares itself for death. [5]

I chose to share this excerpt because it speaks to several relevant issues. It weds religious symbols with the essence of our human psychological nature. As educators we have taken a separatist attitude in regards to religion and psychology, which the study of death, loss, and grief will transcend. We are in an era that warrants a marriage of theology and psychology for a deeper understanding into human behavior. Also, this excerpt shares the belief that neurosis is a state of alienation from our soul. And, last but not least, this example validates death as the natural process of our physical existence and recognizes that death is the fulfillment of life's meaning.

This helps us to understand that not only is death inevitable, but a necessary part of the journey of the soul. It seems to me that all the great religions speak to the transformation of death as having sacred significance and that life in the material world is about the struggle of obtaining the ultimate position of Eternal Grace. Neither Jung nor I am the only witnesses to this. As a perpetual student of the human mystery, I continually read that all ancient and perennial wisdom, as well as contemporary works, acknowledge this inevitable reality.

I am blessed to have such wise mentors and guides: transpersonal psychologist Ken Wilber and theologian Thomas Moore. Wilber and Moore (though I only know them through their writings) have become my spiritual teachers on unity consciousness and the mysteries of the soul. I am grateful for their contributions as one can tell that I have borrowed many of their ideologies and language to express what is in my mind, heart, and soul.

Wilber's devotion to Buddhism has been an enlightened example and is indirectly responsible for leading me back to my family religion of Catholicism. After reading several of Wilber's works eight years ago, and while taking a course in comparative religion, I went on a spiritual journey and educational expedition to a Zen retreat. Having some trouble sitting Zazen due to my spinal cord injury, I found a comfortable alternative position. The deep breathing and mental focus relaxed me completely. The spoken words of wisdom enlightened and warmed my soul. However, I could not bring myself to bow my body in reverence at the alter of the great Buddha statue. I almost had an anxiety attack as I heard a voice in my head say, "Thou shall not have strange gods before Me." This awareness that I was comfortable only bowing with such sacred reverence to the Christ Jesus made me realize that I was not only Catholic by birth,

Irish heritage, and cultural indoctrination, but that Catholicism was indeed the religion manifested by my soul in this lifetime.

From that moment on I began to honor Buddha and the man Jesus as I do all great mystics, prophets, and teachers—with respect and awe. I left the retreat knowing that Catholicism was a choice and where I belong, even though I disagree with some of its patriarchal mandates. I now walk forward in reverence of all religions and spiritual philosophies, knowing that they all have at their root the same message. This message is about love, compassion, acceptance, selflessness, detachment, forgiveness, equality, and ONE...NESS or a union of opposites—a one...ness that transcends our material ego-self and offers a coming together in a spirit of unity consciousness or an emergence with the presence of God.

This complete union of opposites is only realized when the mortal soul is released from the physical body at death and becomes the immortal soul. Life or living is a journey of experiencing both worlds, necessitating grief or angst of the physical world, as well as grace, which is of the spiritual or Divine. Living presents us with the dualistic concepts of heaven and hell, whereas death returns us to wholeness transcending our dualistic nature. We then become ONE with pure consciousness or God.

In his book, *Grace and Grit*, Ken Wilber shares with us a discussion on perennial philosophy, which speaks to my point. He says:

> *In fact, the individual self or ego is precisely what blocks the realization of the Supreme Identity in the first place. Rather, the "you" in question is the deepest part of you— or, if you wish, the highest part of you—the subtle essence, as the Upanishad put it, that transcends your mortal ego and directly partakes of the Divine. In Judaism it is called the ruach, the divine and supraindividual spirit in each and every person, and not the nefesh, or individual ego. In Christianity, it is the indwelling pneuma or spirit that is of one*

essence with God, and not the individual psyche or soul,
which at best can worship God. As Coomaraswamy said,
the distinction between a person's immortal-eternal spirit and
a person's individual-mortal soul (meaning ego) is a fun-
damental tenet of the perennial philosophy.[6]

Gateway to Human Emotions

From the brilliant writings of Thomas Moore, I have learned
that it is not necessary to define the soul, but to accept that it is
real and recognize that, like a dream, it is full of meaning.[7] I
believe it is the gateway to understanding human emotions and
feelings, thus influencing behavior. The soul is not tangible and
does not have materialistic qualities or physical properties; but
it must be respected if we are to understand the pain and suffer-
ing of the human experience. Like the reality of consciousness
and unconsciousness, the soul is of sacred design and full of
mystery. We mortals stand in awe of the simplicity, as well as
the heavenly grandeur of these mysteries.

39

Our conscious and unconscious minds present many symbols
and images for us to explore meaning and purpose within the
human experience. These symbols and images are transported
to us in both the waking and dream states. From Moore's wis-
dom, I gather that the answer is not so much about arriving at
an intellectual definition or logical explanation as it is in the
awareness of the searching, the presence of the imagination,
and the honoring of the ordinary that we discover we are the
living truth. In his book *Care of the Soul*, Moore states:

> *The images, dreams, and experiences that are important to*
> *us will always have a multitude of possible readings and*
> *interpretations, because they are rich with imagination and*
> *soul. I understand that this approach to imagination goes*
> *against the part of us that longs for a conclusion and a*

destination in our search for meaning. This is another reason why care of the soul, in contrast to understanding the soul, amounts to a new paradigm for our modern way of life. It asks us to make a complete turnaround in our usual efforts to figure things out, suggesting a different set of values and new techniques in which we actually appreciate and enjoy the endless unraveling of meaning, the infinitely rich and deep layering of poetics within the shifting, fluid fabric of experience. The desire to squeeze a single meaning out of a dream, or a work of art or a tale from life is inherently and profoundly Promethean. We want to steal fire from the gods for the sake of humanity. We want to replace divine mystery with human rationality. But this loss of complexity and mystery in our everyday response to life stories entails a loss of soul as well, because soul always manifests itself in mystery and multiplicity. [8]

40

I see the human experience as a sacred mystery that is perhaps not to be understood totally but revered for both its simplistic nature and its multitude of evolving components. For some of us this may require blind faith, for others an acceptance that they don't have all the answers. It is certainly about acceptance to one degree or another, an acceptance that we, as humans, are mere players in a more profound orchestration of ALL LIFE.

I explain to my clients and students that it is by having reverence for the human soul that we can appreciate life with all its absurdities. The soul expresses itself in many forms. I hear it in music and in poetry. I see its image in art, nature, and the eyes of my children. I smell its scent in flowers and good food. I feel its warmth in the arms of my lover. And, I taste its bitterness and sweetness each time I witness the story of a bereaved client who has recently lost a loved one.

Our feelings and emotions dwell in the land of the soul which cries out in pain or rejoices with laughter and merriment to express its needs. We must listen with our heart as sometimes the voice of the soul is too subtle to be recognized by our five senses. Gary Zukav, author of *The Seat of the Soul* and *Dancing Wu Lei Masters*, explains that we are evolving to multisensory beings, a condition that goes far beyond our five-sense state of perceptiveness.

I know we are now, more than ever before, in need of being guided by our other senses of intuition, intention, attention, imagination, perception, karma, appreciation, somatic awareness, compassion, and love. I call these our *Esoteric-Sensory-Mediums*.™ They are available to all of us, always have been and always will be. We lost track of them somewhere in our state of time-bound awareness. At this point in my growth, I see intuition, intention, karma, imagination, attention, and appreciation as being of the soul. I understand that perception and somatic-awareness is of the mind-body connection; but that spark or AH-HA that identifies us as the thinker and feeler of the experience is magical. I know mature love and compassion as being of the heart, as they are pure and come from the Divine Spirit or God.

I recognize emotions and feelings as voices or expressions of the soul, which at their zenith are related to the heart. But they are pulled by both negative and positive energies because they are of both worlds. I have come to know that it is through our feelings and emotions that we can bring about balance and harmony. We must nurture and minister to the soul and all its manifestations if we are to realize psychological health and wholeness. I see this in a Taoistic light of trying to maintain a balance. An example of this would be the Yin/Yang concept that has its polarities, yet its oneness and wholeness. We learn to waver through the oscillating currents of the emotional continuum with fear, dread, and anxiety at one end and peace, compassion, and love at the other end. This is the BOTH/AND pendulum of emotionality that moves the spirit of humanity.

My intent as a counselor and teacher in the area of loss and grief is not to overload the client/student with an in-depth study

41

of philosophy and psychological theory, but to offer explanations that I find relevant and to give each individual the opportunity to explore this vast mystery for his/her own truths. We each are at a different level of development and awareness; therefore, it would be inappropriate and presumptuous of me to suggest that I have the answers for others.

When philosopher and theologian Paul Tillich asks the question "And if one is not able to die, is he really able to live?"[9] he gives voice to my new awareness of the paradox that it is through finding meaning and beauty in the natural transformation of death, meaning overcoming our dread and anxiety of this resurrection, that we are more able to live life to the fullest; and, through understanding and transcending our ordinary losses, those we experience every day, we are better prepared to die. My hope is that my ideas will challenge others to begin or to deepen their own exploration, as I am convinced that this type of discovery is necessary to find and maintain health and balance, both psychologically and physically. My premise emphasizes that this exploration is an ongoing process of self-discovery as well as one's connection to the universe.

In the next chapter I share what I have learned about the grief process. Grief is the normal human response to loss, whether due to death or quasi-psychospiritual losses of the human journey. My understanding of the emotionality inherent in the manifestations of grief is fundamental to my concept of healing the soul through ministering to the more ordinary experiences of separation and anxiety.

Do not be afraid of being witnesses to
the dignity of every human being, from
the moment of conception until death.
—His Holiness, Pope John Paul II

4

Discovering the Grief Process

> *There comes a midnight hour when all must unmask.*
>
> —*Soren Kierkegaard*

> *Weeping bitterly, mourning fully, pay tribute to sorrow, as he deserves, then compose yourself after your grief, for grief can bring on an extremity and heart-ache, destroy one's health. For him it was yesterday, for you it is today.*
>
> —*Ecclesiastes 38:17*

As I stated earlier, grief is the normal human response to loss. Loss is a state of being deprived of something one values. Though loss is universal, it has individual meaning be-cause we each have unique personalities that perceive the mean-ing and value of things differently. I have proposed that we come to this material realm as we separate from the bliss of being one in a union of opposites with unity consciousness. Here we find our innate sense of searching for wholeness or need to return to our oneness with God. This by no means implies that life in this natural world is of lesser importance.

Our life, our human beingness, is a sacred gift from the uni-verse. It is our connection to all that is. It is our opportunity for exploration and growth so that we may know that which is God.

We cannot recognize grace if we have nothing to compare it to. If we do not know hell, we cannot revere heaven. If we do not know sorrow, we cannot feel joy. If we are not conscious of death, we cannot truly celebrate life. This paradox is part of the perennial philosophy. The value and/or meaning we place on life, and then on all other attachments, will determine our response of grieving for that which we must lose in order to grow and finally return to wholeness.

There are many losses in the human experience. My study takes a look at those losses which evoke the most stress and anxiety throughout our life span. Grief manifests itself in many ways and to varying degrees. As death is perhaps the greatest sense of loss for most people, and because the study of death and grieving the loss of a loved one were the major components of my healing process, I begin my discussion on grief with what I have learned from those who have shared their transformation of the dying process. I hope my reader will discover, as I have, that we can apply this wisdom to the more ordinary losses of our physical world.

East Meets West

My exploration and understanding of grief is both an eclectic and a holistic perspective. All countries and cultures have their own beliefs, rituals, and customs which assist them through death and the grieving process. From my research, reading, and exploration of the subject, I believe that we in the United States have more difficulty coping with these issues than do other cultures. However, I know that we learn from each other, as I believe we all are students and, at the same time, we all are teachers. Therefore, I hope my awareness will be universally contemplated as I continue learning from the wisdom of all traditions. Now, more than ever before, we are a global community. It is to our advantage to integrate our teachings, benefiting all of humanity.

An example of this would be a message from renowned lecturer and Buddhist spiritual master, Sogyal Rinpoche in his profound interpretation of Tibetan Buddhism's understanding on the mystery of life and death. I am inspired by his work entitled *The Tibetan Book of Living and Dying* and consider it a spiritual work of art. Sogyal Rinpoche says:

> *People who are grieving go through a kind of death. Just like a person who is actually dying, they need to know that the disturbing emotions they are feeling are natural. They need to know too that the process of mourning is a long and often tortuous one, where grief returns again and again in cycles. Their shock and numbness and disbelief will fade, and will be replaced by a deep and at times desperate awareness of the immensity of their loss, which itself will settle eventually into a state of recovery and balance. Tell them that this is a pattern that will repeat itself over and over again, month after month, and that all their unbearable feelings and fears, of being unable to function as a human being any more, are normal. Tell them that although it may take one year or two, their grief will definitely reach an end and be transformed into acceptance.[1]*

45

This passage concurs with Western thought that grief is a natural and normal process. In my mind, the repetition of the waves of emotionality that ebb and flow is analogous to an oscillating spiral of feelings which can emerge from unconsciousness, our soul, and our heart when least expected and without warning. As we consciously process and feel our emotions and choose to move through them, then and only then do we come to a place of acceptance and give ourselves the gift of moving forward to a new consciousness of renewed heart and soul with love and compassion. I have designed a *Spiral of Grief* ™ that demonstrates this ongoing reality, which will be discussed in Chapter Eight.

Rinpoche also points out another important component of this process. He warns us that it may take a year or two for this process through grief before reaching a transformation of letting go and transcending our psychological pain and suffering. It is when we reach this state of grace that we bring our psyche back into harmony and balance.

I cannot state strongly enough one truism: There is no universal time schedule for the grief process. It may take some individuals six months or less while it may take others two years or more. It takes as long as it takes! It is important that we honor each bereaved individual his/her own time to heal. However, as has been said many times before by my hospice colleagues, time alone is a slow healer and, in my opinion, a dangerous one. Time alone is not what healing is about. It is what *we do* with our time that rewards us with a sense of acceptance so that we can move forward with our lives. Otherwise, unresolved, deep grief—that intense pain of loss and separation—invades the human organism like a cancer that manifests as pathological neurosis and psychosis or splintering of the soul.

The Tibetan philosophy offers a deep understanding into the paradox of life and death acknowledging that it is through understanding death that we learn to celebrate life. It is through our pain and suffering that we learn to recognize joy, ecstasy, peace, and enlightenment. Reading and understanding the wisdom of Sogyal Rinpoche was key in developing my awareness that both life and death are about change. If we are not open to enlightenment or expansion of consciousness, we can remain stuck in our pain. When this happens, we are victims of the darker side of the soul which interferes with our automatic reactions and our conscious taking of action (behaviors) in our living.

I know that, by giving ourselves permission to grieve and by feeling the darker needs of the soul, we finally arrive at the lighter, more joyous side. Just as death is about change, so is life about change. This one law in the universe that never changes—that all things change and are impermanent—is paradoxically the truth of pain and suffering. It is when we are present with or witness to our pain and suffering that we are graced with the liberty to celebrate life.[2]

In the West we have the good fortune of learning from the wisdom of Elisabeth Kubler-Ross. Kubler-Ross has spent the past thirty-five years or so tending to the souls of the dying as they face their fears of transcending this known, physical world to the vast, unknown mysteries of the other world. As she listens with her heart, she is able to hear the voice of the soul which cries out in fear and doubt during this sacred passage.

Her writings and the mission of the hospice movement have been directly responsible for my realization that it is the dignity of human life, the respect for life, the quality not quantity of time that one spends participating in this collective physical realm of living that is of greatest importance. This philosophy helps us to balance out the suffering of losing someone we love. If we can remember to cherish their presence on this earth, celebrate the attachment or relationship which we shared with them, and hold their spirit deep in our memories and hearts after they are gone, then, our pain will be more tolerable.

Elisabeth Kubler-Ross is most noted and referenced for her knowledge of the dying process, which she sums up in her book *On Death and Dying* as: (1) denial and isolation, (2) anger, (3) bargaining, (4) depression, and (5) acceptance.[3] Grief experts Judy Tatelbaum, Judith Viorst, David Dietrich and Peter Shabad, and others who share their perspectives on loss have used Kubler-Ross's awareness as foundational theory for the grieving process. As an educator and grief counselor, I accept their wisdom and take this model even further in exploring all the psychological changes in life. Judith Viorst author of *Necessary Losses*, and Dietrich and Shabad, authors of *The Problems of Loss and Mourning*, also correlate loss to life experiences other than death.

The most valuable lesson I learned from Kubler-Ross was the insight and practice of listening with both heart and mind. I have come to know that the greatest gift that we can give to anyone is being present in spirit, attentive of mind, and listening with the heart. When we truly listen in this way, there is no judgement, only unconditional love.

I rarely give advice, but on this important issue I will. The most valuable counsel I can offer anyone who is professionally or personally assisting someone with grief is to practice the art of silence and of listening reverently and devotedly. One's presence with intentions of love is all that is necessary, especially in the early stages of grief. As mourners come through their intense emotional pain and mental confusion of these earlier phases and begin to reconstruct their lives, it then becomes appropriate to exchange stories and mirror back to the bereaved his/her thoughts and feelings.

When I was involved with hospice I ministered to a family at my local hospital who had just received the news that their daughter/sister had committed suicide. The family and I were strangers to one another, and this was my first direct involvement with a suicide case. As I held them in my arms and absorbed their emotional and physical pain into my heart, soul, and body, I prayed to God to give me the wisdom to say the right thing. I spent three hours tending to the sadness of their souls and during all this time—except for announcing that I was a hospice bereavement volunteer—I said only, "What can I do to help you?" The rest of the time I was silent. God had answered my prayers.

From her book *The Courage To Grieve*, Judy Tatelbaum shares with us:

> *A grieving friend needs our friendship and support to go*
> *through and complete the mourning process. We must reach*
> *out and take the initiative in offering help. The most valu-*

able thing we have to give is our presence. It is far more important than our knowledge or our advice, for the companionship of family and friends is the greatest source of support and solace. We can help our grieving friend most by sitting near, holding a hand, giving a hug, passing a tissue, crying together, listening, sharing our feelings. In other words, what the bereaved need most is our acknowledgement of their pain and sorrow. And we both must realize that we cannot erase that pain. In coping with loss, the bereaved are greatly depleted of energy. The presence of others helps energize and renew them. Sometimes mourners feel a drop in energy when guests depart, as if it is other people who almost literally hold them up.[4]

I left the hospital that day after the arrival of my new clients' support system. Intuitively, I knew that the presence and embrace of their family and friends was what they needed. In her message we hear Tatelbaum speaking to the importance of *acknowledgement*. When we acknowledge or bear witness to someone else's pain and suffering, we are giving the gift of compassion. This shows respect for their human beingness. It is their process, not ours. We are there only to offer and demonstrate love.

In their book *The Problems of Loss and Mourning: Psychoanalytic Perspectives*, Dietrich and Shabad explore the similarities and differentiate between object loss and body loss. They recognize the creativity of the soul in dealing with body loss or the experience of "phantom limb."[5] Their discussion makes us aware of the ongoing subjective/objective dualistic nature of the human condition. Whether we lose an object of the external world (a loved one due to death or divorce, our home in a fire, or a job due to corporate downsizing) or an object of the subjective physical self (such as a loss of sight, an amputated leg, or the use of a kidney), we go through a profound sense of loss which must be grieved in order to bring the psyche back into healthy balance.

Loss of any nature must be replaced. The human organism interacting with the human spirit is resilient. This resiliency creates a means of restoration that is also a process of tending to or healing the soul. My personal experiences of divorce (loss of a love object) and that of breaking my neck (body loss) which resulted in loss of physical movement and a reality of living in daily pain, substantiates the resiliency and creativeness of the Holistic Self. It was my awareness and ability to grieve these different losses that restored me to wholeness. While my perspective recognizes that these losses (object-body) are different, I know the grieving process is similar in both instances. As we continue to mature and experience living, we create new ways of coping with our life situations.

Grief, Stress, and Anxiety

There are many terms that we use in place of *grief*. One might use the synonyms of *sorrow, sadness, regret, vexation, dolor, misery, anguish, anxiety, woe, heartache, pain, lament, despair, agony*, and the list goes on and on.[6] Actually, many of the above terms are symptoms or manifestations of grief. For the purpose of education and in the interest of psychological study, I suggest that the word *grief* is equal to and is appropriately interchangeable with the terms *mourning* and *bereavement* for a death loss, and appropriately interchangeable with *stress, anxiety*, and *trauma* for other losses of living and life transitions.

Grieving, mourning, and bereavement suggest in their meanings that this state of being is a process. One of the most important tenets of my paradigm is that this human response to loss is a process, not an event in our lives. This is key because of the truth that grief, in all its forms, comes in waves throughout our entire life. Its degree of intensity fluctuates and spirals in and out of our everyday beingness. Our emotions and feelings interact with the soma (meaning body), our consciousness, and the brain which together play havoc with the entire human organism. As we minister to the needs of our emotional soul, we bring our whole being back into a place of homeostasis or balance.

The manifestations of grief become less intense as we realize a mystical and powerful sense of strength and courage that carries us forward in a new light. Supporting the BOTH/AND concept, we begin to understand that our living journey is about a glorious and humble awareness and appreciation for the emergence of inner contentment, joy, and ecstasy that has been actualized only because we have been in and through the abyss of pain and darkness.

I see grief as having several categories. The first is *collective grief* which is a community response to a tragic event with its many levels of loss. The Oklahoma City bombing, the Challenger Mission of 1986, and the assassinations of President John F. Kennedy, Martin Luther King Jr., and, more recently, Israel's Prime Minister Yitzak Rabin are examples of this type of grief. Our nation's children are quietly committing suicide or taking out their depression and anger on their classmates and teachers. Our communities are in great distress over the school shootings of the past five years. Within events of this nature, we recognize individual, national, and global mourning. Grief has a ripple effect, both individually and collectively.

Ripple Effect

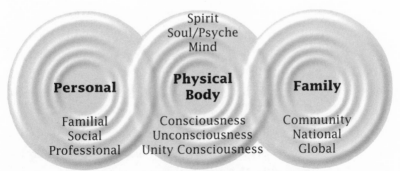

Ripple Effect illustrating a holistic approach to the emotionality of loss and grief.

Grief touches each individual to varying degrees, ranging from mild sadness to the darkest depths of posttraumatic stress. Individually, it can affect our personal, familial, social, and professional lives. As expressions of the soul our feelings affect our material self, social self, and spiritual self. They manifest in all realms of beingness: physical, mental, conscious awareness and unconsciousness, soul or psyche, and at the level of spirit. The metaphor of a ripple effect provides an understanding into the complex and multifaceted reality of grief. And, within each of these components, we discover varying degrees of effect which are overlapping, splashing into each other like the waves of an oceanic storm. As Sogyal Rinpoche poetically stated: "The realm of deep grief is samsara or an ocean of unbearable suffering."[7]

The second category of grief is *individual grief.* This is your grief and yours alone. When someone dies there are many survivors as each human being has his/her attachments to many others. The degree of pain, the individual's truth, depends upon the relationship of each mourner to the deceased. We need to allow each individual his/her own pain no matter what position in the relationship he/she occupied. A spousal attachment, the parent-child symbiosis, the inseparableness of siblings, the intertwinement of lovers and dear friends, and the loss of a devoted pet are those losses that most effectively disturb our sense of wholeness and feelings of being complete.

The manifestations of loss and grief affect our entire sense of being and touch or ripple out into every aspect of our lives. We may have trouble concentrating on our studies or work. We can feel depleted of spirit and faith. We may experience physical symptoms like headaches or nausea. Sometimes we close off our emotions and distance ourselves from family and friends. Grief affects every part of us and our interactions with everyone around us. When our sense of wholeness has been splintered, our soul is there to bring us back into balance. Remember, the soul is of both worlds, the physical and the spiritual, and it has within its power the dualistic nature of both fear and love and all degrees of emotionality in between. When we recognize and tend to the emotional needs of our soul, we become empowered to expand our consciousness, which results in a dissipation of our pain and suffering.

When an individual experiences multiple losses, the intensity of the suffering is greater. *Compounded grief* is the third category and manifests itself in various situations. We may lose more than one loved one at the same time due to accidental death or divorce. Or the experience may present itself as the death of several loved ones within a short period of time. For example, if we lose a grandparent to death in May of one year and a parent, child, or someone else with whom we have a close loving bond in October or November of the same year, our grief is compounded due to the recurrence of loss within such a short time. Also, our losses are multiple and our grief is compounded if we lose someone to the transformation of death while at the same time or soon after we experience other losses or psychological changes in our lives—the more ordinary separations caused by developmental growth stages, divorce, drug and alcohol abuse, job loss, etc. (I will speak to these losses in the next few chapters).

The fourth category of grief is a two-sided coin. Common sense tells us that loss happens either expectedly, with some degree of advanced warning and awareness, or that it happens unexpectedly, out of the blue. So, on one side of the coin we will experience *anticipatory grief*, as happens with terminal illness, and on the other side we have *unforeseen grief*. What I have learned by listening to clients and students, referring to the hundreds of case studies I have read, and relying on my own personal experiences strongly suggests that sudden or unexpected loss and death produce the most stress, anxiety, and trauma. The human organism has not been prepared for this separation and therefore suffers to a different degree. Grief, pain, and suffering are difficult and every human being has my respect in determining his/her own degree of attachment and pain.

Many of us experience what I call *ongoing* or *prolonged grief*, category number five. This is continuing stress and anxiety exacerbated by the presence of other loss issues. It occurs when we deal with illnesses or conditions for extended periods of time—for example when caring for someone with Alzheimer's, or having to live daily with chronic pain. The individual suffering, their families, and their caretakers go through a grief that seems to linger for years until that person finally makes the transition to the other world. The families who live with physical and/or mental disabilities, poverty, racism, and other forms of oppression and victimization have ongoing grief resulting from the stress and anxiety they endure daily. Their symptoms of helplessness and hopelessness may last a lifetime.

These categories of grief, (1) collective, (2) individual, (3) compounded, (4) anticipatory and/or unforeseen, and (5) ongoing or prolonged, are normal human reactions to loss. They apply to the dying process, the loss of a loved one to death, and the many losses of living. It is important that people know they are not going crazy and they are not alone. We need to recognize and tend to the emotionality of the soul if we are to move forward. We cannot do this by ourselves. We should not only give ourselves permission to minister to our soul's needs, but we must invite or welcome others to assist us through this process.

There is a sixth category of grief which we fall into all too often. It is *unresolved grief*. This happens when we individually or collectively ignore or deny the pain and suffering of the soul. If we do not work through our grief, it remains suppressed or repressed in every living cell of our body, which darkens the human spirit. I know that unresolved grief affects us physically, psychologically, mentally, socially, and spiritually. It will fester until it destroys the human organism in one way or another. We must learn to gently unmask or peel back the layers of psychological pain and suffering as we would remove the thistles and leaves of the artichoke to get to the core essence or heart of our human beingness. If we do not cultivate the conscious mind, minister to the needs of the soul, and nurture our human heart, we lose our connection to the Spirit and continue to suffer.

This first section has been dedicated to exploring the meaning of life and death and the grieving process that goes with the loss of a loved one. I believe that we can apply this awareness to healing the soul around the more ordinary experiences of loss and separation, and the resulting stress, anxiety, and trauma of living in this physical realm. Our challenge remains one of loving, letting go, and moving forward towards the light of pure consciousness as we live in this physical world. Accepting the challenges of life, we encounter all the emotions of the soul. Our responsibility becomes that of managing our feelings in a constructive manner so as not to hurt ourselves or others, but to become living examples of love and compassion. Section Two discusses the psychological application of loss and grief as it correlates with the emotionality of living. The areas of loss which will be covered are (1) developmental stages and life transitions, (2) divorce and relationship issues, (3) physical and mental challenges, (4) drug and alcohol abuse, (5) terminal illness, and (6) other losses in life.

55

Soren Kierkegaard told us "There comes a midnight hour when all must unmask." Please do not wait for the midnight hour of death to unmask and discover the heart of your human beingness. I believe that it is by accepting the challenge of living in the presence of our soul and listening with our hearts that we learn to celebrate life for today and all our tomorrows.

And ever has it been that love knows not
its own depth until the hour of separation.
—Kahlil Gibran

Section Two

Celebrating the Human Experience

The ultimate cure, as many ancient and modern psychologies of depth have asserted, comes from love and not from logic.

—Thomas Moore

5

Development of the Holistic Self

*The Soul is our house; our eyes, its
windows; and our words, its messenger.*
—Kahlil Gibran

*Our task is to find a way to weave deep-
seated emotions into our daily lives; to
clothe eternity in the garments of time.*
—Thomas Moore

In this chapter, I share psychological theory and other concepts
that I find helpful in understanding loss and grief in relationship to
the developing psyche. There are many alternative theories available
and I encourage my readers to put my work in a context that is most
comfortable for them. Using my holistic paradigm of mind-body-
soul-spirit, I will speak to the various stages of the developing self.

In Chapter One, I referenced William James' model of the *self*
as having several systems which are intrinsically woven together
forming the complexity of the individual human experience. This
holistic model takes into account the subjective and objective
(I-Me) realm of awareness and as sacred psychologist Jean Hous-
ton would say, much, much more. The three aspects of the "Me"
are the material or physical self, the social self, and the spiritual
self (the self as Known), which together with the "I" (the self as
Knower) form a whole or holy self which is more than the sum
of its parts. I refer to this as the Holistic Self.

To illustrate this we can consider a house. Within a house there are many rooms that are subsets of the whole house. Each room is composed of another set of subqualities, which include the windows, walls, ceilings and floors. This subset is made up of other unique materials such as nails, mortar, wood, brick, etc. Also, there are different levels of the house: the basement (or foundation), the main floor (or working-growing-changing space), and the additional, upper floor or attic which is the highest level of architectural design.

To this objective environment we add the subjectiveness of each member who resides in this time-space awareness. Even though each person has his/her own unique personalities, we group them together and refer to them as a family, biological or surrogate. Collectively, this unification of systems and subsystems is known as a home. This aggregate has a complex meaning which is much, much more than the sum of its parts. If we keep this analogy in mind as we explore the development of the individual or *self*, we will discover a deeper meaning of the human condition. 59

Historically, the science of psychology has studied human behavior through different lenses. The foundation of psychology goes back to antiquity and is rooted in the philosophies of Plato, Aristotle, Descartes, and Locke. Seventeenth century English philosopher John Locke believed that when we are born, the human mind is *tabula rasa* or a blank slate. Today, most psychologists would disagree with this theory, recognizing that even in vitro there is an emotional sense of at least pain an pleasure. As we evolve, so do our sciences. From each branch of science, many areas of specialization have emerged. My position is an eclectic one as I abstract ideas from all areas of science including biology, psychology, physiology, and sociology. I also draw from the humanities, including history, philosophy, mythology, and theology.

To understand loss and grief, stress, and the human psyche's sense of separation and anxiety, we do not have to be a scholar or an expert in any one or all of these disciplines. I trust that we have evolved to a place of high intelligence with observant characteristics that enable each of us to grasp my message phenomenologically. Though we all have different experiences and are at different levels of development, one universal truth is that we all experience loss as well as the emotional reactions to loss. Also, we are united by the spirit of humanity, which is resilient and present to assist us. These common denominators give us each the level of understanding that we need to recognize our heart and soul so as to heal our pain and suffering.

As I lecture on the important issue of the emotionality of the soul, I offer my students psychological theory and philosophic ideas, and give them the opportunity to share their personal experiences. This format allows them to bring their unique wisdom to our discussions as we explore the mystery together. I believe that education and awareness emerge through the sharing of knowledge and experience. Also, I feel we are on the horizon of witnessing the marriage of psychology, in its many forms, with spirituality. Spirituality is BOTH a sacred AND individual freedom of the highest order of evolution.

Development of the Holistic Self or the whole person is a journey of constant change and growth. We go from attachment (connecting), to detachment (letting go), and eventually to transcendence or moving forward from one state of being to another. This cycle is ongoing and recurring throughout the human life span. As the soul separates from the Divine Spirit, it connects with the material realm by attaching to the womb of humanity via a mystery or miracle, which science does not yet understand. As the physical or material self grows from the immaturity of the zygote to the maturity of a fully developed fetus, the natural world gives birth to a human being. We all know that during the first few years of life, we go through many physical, mental, emotional, spiritual, and social changes. As we accept each new challenge we let go of the security and comfort of the previous state of existence. I will not go into the stages of physical development except to acknowledge that it takes place

60

naturally and with it comes a psychological process of attach-
ment and acceptance to each new stage of physical beingness,
and a letting go or detachment from the previous body image.

An Integration of Theory

For several reasons, I am most comfortable with the Eight-
Stage model of psychosocial development offered by twentieth
century, post-Freudian, Erik Erikson. First, Erikson's model is
more inclusive than Freud's psychosexual model of development,
Sullivan's interpersonal theory, or Piaget's theory of cognitive
development. These earlier theories stopped short of adulthood
and neglected the unfolding of the more mature person. I know
that we continue to develop until we die. A more progressive
model is needed, especially in regards to loss and grief. It is in
the autumn of life that we have equally important challenges
and rewards of change and transformation.

Secondly, Erikson's model speaks to the physical, psychologi-
cal, and social aspects of human beingness. He extends Freud's
psychoanalytical theory and his approach is more holistic and
better parallels my paradigm of mind-body-soul-spirit. My con-
cept of the developing Holistic Self goes beyond the ego-self to
encompass the soul of humanity in an individual and collective
spirit of what I call *community consciousness*.

Erikson's eight stages range from birth to death in the follow-
ing order:
- Basic Trust versus Mistrust (0-1 year)
- Autonomy versus Shame and Doubt (1-3 years)
- Initiative versus Guilt (3-5 years)
- Industry versus Inferiority (5-11years)
- Identity versus Role Confusion (11-18 years)
- Intimacy versus Isolation (18-40 years)
- Generativity versus Stagnation (40-65 years)
- Integrity versus Despair (65 and older)

61

In my discussion of the loss or separation and anxiety that is inherent throughout the developing or evolving psyche, I integrate Erik Erikson's concepts of psychosocial development and humanistic psychologist Abraham Maslow's theory of human motivation.[1] Through this synthesis, I hope to arrive at a more comprehensive view of emotional and spiritual human growth and development. Known globally as Maslow's *Hierarchy of Needs*, the motives include:

- Biological Needs
- Safety Needs
- Love and Belongingness
- Self-Esteem
- Self-Actualization

Maslow noted that each stage must be met in order to move forward to a higher place of psychological growth. This is true in healing our losses. If early losses are not grieved and transcended, then we carry them internally where they do all sorts of damage to the living organism. This is what is known as compounded grief.

At the end of his career, Maslow extended his theory of becoming self-actualized to include transcendence, meaning the spiritual realm, and he referred to these experiences as *Being or B-values*. Also, he recognized that the stages of motivation were not necessarily progressive. Motivation is cyclical and not always age specific. When an individual loses his/her job or becomes homeless, he/she loses his/her safety of income, hearth, and home, making it difficult to reach his/her fullest potential. We see this reality every day as we witness the social welfare system.

When we are trapped in a microcosm where there is no respect for individual souls, we become oppressed, depressed, and helpless, with no sense of dignity, identity, and self-worth. Often we are forced "back to work" in a job that pays less and offers fewer benefits, like childcare, than we received on public assistance. The powers that be must reevaluate our current system to help those in troubled times. Many American women and children are suffering unnecessarily. This is not acceptable in the wealthiest and most powerful nation in the world. There is so much psychological and spiritual pain and suffering in this segment of society as they struggle with the oppression of poverty, helplessness, and hopelessness, which creates a multitude of issues of prolonged loss and grief.

Loss Through Development

From the first breaths of life until eighteen months of age, it is imperative that each individual receive an abundance of love and attention. As parents or guardians, we must tend to the material/physical needs of our children, as well as minister to and nurture their hearts and soul. We do this by warm embrace, gentle touch, and sweetness of voice, which are just as important as a comfortable and warm living environment and adequate and nutritious food. Consistency and continuity are crucial for the infant in developing a sense of *trust*. Abraham Maslow would call this a fulfillment of our *biological* or basic human *needs*. Research proves that infants respond to and thrive with human touch and warm embrace.

63

If the infant's needs are not met, then the child automatically suffers emotional loss and grief. Many children in our country go unattended. They live in unsafe environments and without proper nutrition. Many are homeless and/or unwanted or unloved. And, of course, there is the reality of physical and sexual abuse of children which is incomprehensible if we see our children as blessings from the other world or gifts of Divine Grace from God. The loss of not getting our basic needs met creates a sense of *mistrust* that develops into states of hopelessness and fear. This splintering of the soul can be irreversible and to the least degree affects the developing personality, behavior, sense of self, and a sense of being alive.

By the age of three, if the child has developed trust with his/her parents, primary caregivers, and the environment then the child begins to explore his/her independence. Developing a sense of the independent self rewards the child with self-control and acceptance of direction from others. When *autonomy* of free choice does not develop, the child often becomes secretive, sneaky, and full of *shame and doubt*. This could be the beginning of what modern psychology refers to as "learned helplessness." We cannot realize our own potential if we are stuck in this stage of excessive shamefulness. This loss of creative individuality further damages the psyche, leaving us incapable of choosing self-restraint and making decisions to apply ourselves. At this age we know nothing about how to grieve this loss, so we act out inappropriately in our behavior or repress a sense of shame that disturbs the maturing psyche. We become doubtful and hesitant.

Parents need to encourage inquisitiveness and the child's exploration of the world to alleviate the development of ambivalence or *guilt*. Between the ages of three and five, we go through a period of self-expansion and exploration into new situations. Children need to learn to take risks, *initiating* some of their own choices. Loss of opportunity in the area of taking chances not only stunts creativity of the soul, but may lead to aggressive or manipulative tendencies. Erikson's model states that during this stage, the developing self begins to recognize the virtue of purpose. If we lose the development of a sense of purposefulness, we lose the courage to pursue goals and instead are haunted by fear of punishment and guilt. The child wonders if it is safe to become himself or herself.

Most child development experts would agree that between the ages of six to eleven, it is important to learn intellectual, social, and physical skills. Any of us who have raised children know that this is the age of acquiring playmates and friends.

Children's peer groups become the judge and jury on how they play, what they play with, and which clothes and accessories they wear. Children compare themselves to their peers and if they feel they matchup, then they develop a sense of belonging, acceptance, and achievement or what Erikson refers to as a sense of *industry*. Erikson says that it is during this stage of life that children develop a sense of competence. If we lose our sense of *love and belonging* (Maslow's third stage of motivation), from either our family or peer group, then we take on feelings of *inferiority*, which can cause emotional pain and suffering for many years, perhaps a lifetime.

The ages of twelve to eighteen are perhaps the most critical stage in developing one's self-identity. This is adolescence and a very confusing stage of development. I personally feel this period of development extends until age twenty-five. If we never develop a true sense of self, then we lose connection to our soul. Psychologically, if we do not form a sense of *identity*, we may spend a lifetime trying to figure out who we are. We are not children, but at the same time we do not feel like adults. Our *roles* are *confusing*, multiple, and conflicting. Also, during this period we fall in love usually for the first time. Our hormones are raging, but we are not yet mature enough to make commitments and become parents.

Loss of identity and loss of *self-esteem* (our sense of worth), Maslow's fourth stage, cause us to behave in inappropriate ways that are damaging to the human spirit and sometimes to our physical bodies as well. This can create a sense of hopelessness and helplessness that we have not been socialized to grieve and transcend. As indicated in Daniel Goleman's book, *Emotional Intelligence*, statistics show high rates of teenage pregnancies, suicide, and drug and alcohol addiction are results of one's concept of self and lack of emotional maturity.[2]

We also see rising cases of eating disorders, anorexia nervosa and/or bulimia nervosa, beginning with dieting during this developmental stage. I lost my eldest sister to anorexia when she died at the young age of forty-two after a twenty-five year battle with her obsession of body image and weight loss. There are many components factoring into this devastating reality of self-abuse, more commonly known as "eating disorders." Whether severe dieting and weight loss or obesity due to obsessive over-eating, these complex conditions are heavily intertwined with loss and grief issues.

With guidance, love, and support from our family and community, most of us survive this period of adolescence and develop into responsible adults. However, I believe that as parents we must teach by example. I personally do not feel that most adults (including myself until age forty) have successfully completed this process of developing a true sense of self and fall short of being able to assist our children in their troubling times of conflicting emotions.

Historically and culturally, we consider individuals to be young adults around the age of eighteen to twenty-one. I suggest changing this stage of early adulthood to twenty-five to forty years of age. The expected life span is approaching one hundred years; therefore, I feel it appropriate to redefine these age categories. This stage is the one in which we develop *intimacy* bonds with self and others, and according to Erikson the virtue of love comes into being. As Robert Crooks and Jean Stein discuss Erikson's psychosocial model of development in their textbook *Psychology, Science, Behavior, Life*, they state: "Failure to achieve intimacy is likely to result in a sense of isolation in which the young adult may be reluctant to establish close ties with anyone else."[3] This is evident in the multimillion-dollar industry of learning to communicate with one's lover or spouse, the self-help phenomenon, and relationship experts who flood the air waves and lecture halls with advice on repairing the damage of not getting our early developmental needs met.

Please do not misunderstand me. I applaud the work of my colleagues who are ministering to the needs of this age group as we all work together to heal the emotional pain and suffering in relationships. This feeling of *isolation* is one I have personally suffered. Also, I know it is a manifestation of grieving that which we lost, or never had, and it must be worked through before we can come to a place of transcending our psychological pain, enabling us to move forward.

The maturing adult is in conflict between self-centeredness or *stagnation* and the healthy development of *generativity*, what Erikson refers to as a time of determining our purpose in life and contributing to the well-being of others. I would define this phase of development as being between the ages of forty and seventy. This is a period of shedding the narcissism of the ego self or peeling back the leaves of the artichoke to rediscover our soul, perhaps knowing our hearts for the first time. I encourage every human being to seriously consider this opportunity for what Maslow would call *self-actualization*. Our gift to our children is in authentically living this reality of development, being an exemplar, and passing on the virtues of care, love, and compassion.

When we do not move beyond the ego-self, we stagnate and lose any further opportunity of personal growth and development. Because we have not been socialized to resolve our grief and express our disappointments around these issues of lost maturity, we remain stuck in our emotional pain, even though this may be unconscious. An example of stagnation can be seen in the "empty nest" syndrome. When their children grow up and leave home, many women feel their purpose in life, motherhood, is over and they do not know what to do with themselves. They must take a risk and step outside their comfort zone, learn new things, and create new interest in further developing their human potential. Likewise, I see this happening to men as they retire. Having identified themselves with their careers for many years, they feel there is no meaning to life once they quit working.

I have a difficult time understanding my peers or contemporaries, other baby boomers, who cannot wait to retire at age fifty-five, and then go golfing for the rest of their life. Golfing and other forms of relaxation are fine; but, we should not make these activities our primary goal. After our children are raised and/or we have retired, there are many productive years left to contribute to the well-being of humanity and the planet. Consider finding a cause and get involved. There is new data proving that seniors who keep active minds and participate in life are healthier and live longer. The autumn of life can be a period of euphoria and joy with a sacred sense of self, purpose, contribution, and a communion with our Holistic Self.

The last stage of the human journey is seen by Erikson as a time when we accept the lifestyle of others while honoring and defending our own choice of lifestyle. We have successfully completed the seven earlier stages of development and perceive our life as having order and meaning within a larger order. For me, this would be an awareness of unity consciousness or a psychological reemergence with the Spirit of God. We have developed *integrity* and enjoy a sense of peace about our journey here on earth.

This time is characterized by extensive reflection in which we come to a place of acceptance or balance of our accomplishments and our failures. We have full awareness of the BOTH/AND concept of living and all its losses and rewards. It is designed by our Creator to be a beautiful and serene state of beingness. If we have not successfully developed to this psychosocial-spiritual zenith, we face a reality of *despair* during our old age. Here we see much sadness and passiveness about our life and we have a difficult time in preparing to die. Despair is also a manifestation of grief that has not been resolved. Symptoms of loss and grief manifest at varying degrees and levels for each of us.

I am convinced that these psychosocial stages of development are important in determining our degree of emotional pain and suffering, and thus our behaviors. All stages of development, change, and transition can be highly charged with emotions that we have not been socialized to handle. In our attempt to recover or heal from any underdeveloped aspects of our Holistic Self, it is imperative that we remember two things. First, this is not about blaming our parents or accusing and confronting them with their lack of child-rearing skills. Each generation does the best that it can do at a particular point of evolution in history, guided by both the prevailing Zeitgeist and individual knowledge and experience. Second, and most important, is our taking responsibility to rediscover our souls and work through our personal losses and grief. We are not only rewarded with a transformation out of our emotional pain and suffering, but we are given the opportunity to be active participants in the collective spirit of humanity.

Each one of us is on a hero's journey, both individually and collectively. It is about learning, letting go, and moving forward. Abraham Maslow would say it is about becoming *self-actualized* and a further transcendence of materialism to spirituality. Twentieth century Neo-Freudian Erich Fromm said, "Man's main task in life is to give birth to himself, to become what he potentially is." Individual human potential is a subset of the divine house of potentiality which governs the whole cosmos. As each of us gives birth to him- or herself, the Holistic Self, we rediscover our "heart and soul" with a present awareness of the spiritual duality of living in both worlds.

69

Sexuality and Spirituality

I would like to address several areas of psychosexual and psychospiritual development that are rarely discussed, but necessary as we study human emotion from the reference point of the soul. Our development of spirituality comes into consciousness around the age of thirteen which parallels the age of sexual development, such as the onset of menses. These rites of passage are honored via various rituals in many religions. In Judaism, this is when young boys and girls mark their transition into manhood and womanhood through the celebration of Bar Mitzvah and Bat Mitzvah respectively. Catholics celebrate this transformation with the sacrament of Confirmation, an acceptance of the "Christ within" which connects us to the Holy Spirit. I remember, shortly after my Zen retreat and subsequent reunification with Catholicism, that I remarked to a friend, "My sense of spirituality seems so simple, clear, and pure — I haven't felt this way since I was twelve or thirteen — the feeling is the same." I knew then what my mission and purpose in life was: to serve God by ministering to the pain and suffering of humanity. How this would manifest, I wasn't sure. But, I knew if I kept my heart open, guidance would come on the wings of angels.

I often think about those who are dealing with conflicting emotions of their sexual identity and sexual preference of partners. I observe a great deal of anxiety, stress, and grief as I encounter individuals who are in psychological denial and torment around issues of living a homosexual lifestyle, rather than the more conventional heterosexual lifestyle. It is not only the individual who suffers. Due to the homophobia in this country, many parents and siblings of bisexual, gay, and lesbian children suffer varying degrees of loss and grief that are hard to work through. We can alleviate much of the mental confusion, despair, isolation, and emotional pain by coming to a place of acceptance around these issues. We must show love, kindness, compassion, and respect for everyone if we are to evolve spiritually.

These issues of development demonstrate my mind-body-soul-spirit paradigm. Biologically and psychologically, we go through radical changes in our physical appearance, with a ripening of sexual hormones, conflict of the emotional soul, mental confusion as to choices and responsibilities, and conscious awareness of *being* a spiritual being. Needless to say, this is one of the most significant yet disturbing epochs of life. I mention this psycho-sexual-spiritual transitions as they clearly illustrate the Both/And...ness of growth and development. As we explore

70

our self-identity and discover a more mature autonomy and independence, we struggle with role confusion and sense loss in the area of detachment from parents and family. We also awaken to our sexual identity and a spiritual connection to a larger family system called humanity and the omnipotent force of our higher self or connection to God.

After marriage and the arrival of children, many couples experience psychosexual difficulties. Sometimes the father has a sense of loss resulting from the time and attention being directed to the newborn. He may lose interest in marital sexual intimacy as he unconsciously thinks of his wife as the archetypal, idealized virgin-mother. He sees her differently now, in the role of mother, not as a lover. He may search for fulfillment of his sexual needs outside the marriage.

Or, it may be the wife who experiences psychosexual dysfunction. As a new mother, and more so with the arrival of additional children, the wife is often too tired and stressed due to a heavy sense of responsibility to enjoy sexual intimacy. Also, her physical body and hormone levels have gone through radical changes. These problems can separate the couple's love bond and often brings them into marriage counseling.

Another traumatic phase in which we experience a great deal of loss occurs during "leaving the nest" for the young adult which results in "the empty nest" for their parents. As grown children leave their family and venture into the unknown world of adulthood, their parents prepare for a change in identity by letting go and redefining life's purpose. My daughter explained to me, after having made this transition, that when she left home to go to UCLA, she experienced a deep sense of loss concerning financial security and the support of her family foundation to lean on. Her words were "There was no going back, only forward." The manifestations of grief for her were sadness, loneliness, depression, and fear.

Many times, parents have more than one child, so their empty nest feeling may not arrive all at once. It may be a gradual

71

transition. Friends and colleagues have shared that once the house was empty and quiet, they wept for days and in some cases weeks. I feel this bond is strongest in the mother-daughter relationship. As mothers we must redefine our sense of purpose when the nest becomes empty. Fathers, also may experience feelings of "empty nest," but I feel this departure creates a greater degree of transition for women, as mothers are still the primary caregivers of children. In any case, this is about becoming our Holistic Self, just on a different level. Who are we and what do we do next are the questions asked by those leaving as well as by those who are left.

Culturally, many of us identify with the reality of "mid-life crisis." This can be a painful time for both males and females. We get lost in regret of our passing youth and fearful of our future or old age and death. Depression is often a symptom of this form of grief. Many of us act out with inappropriate behavior and lifestyles trying to recapture our lost youth. Personally, during this stage I was healing my unmet infant and adolescent needs and, as a result, witnessed what transpersonal psychologist Christina Grof would call a *spiritual emergency*.[4] As I quit drinking and began to live the twelve-step philosophy, I suffered a deep sense of loss around the person I had portrayed for forty years. I was not sure how to go forward. Plunging into the study of various religions, reading everything I could get my hands on, learning to meditate (a practice I continue to this day), and visiting the Sonoma Mountain Zen Center all were instrumental in bringing me home to a renewed sense of the "Christ within" myself. This was a slow process, a five-year rebirth. I experienced a loss of one part of self, feeling void of spirit; and, I discovered a newer part of self that connected me to a greater sense of unity consciousness and a reunification with God. Letting go of my earlier-formed identity, my socialized ego-self, and all my defense mechanisms granted me the grace of serenity. Reflection and mindful contemplation rewarded me with new insights, meaning, and purpose. I am blessed to have come through this transition with a renewed sense of self; I now walk forward in a light of hope with peace of mind and reverence of soul.

From birth and until death, the human psyche goes through many inevitable stages of change. These quasi-deaths of the soul bring a sense of loss which we must grieve if we are to enjoy mental, physical, psychological, and spiritual health. Coping effectively and managing our emotions through these various transitions of the human journey will assist us in realizing optimal health and better prepare us to handle our transformation to the other world. The truth is that understanding death teaches us how to live, and living in the presence of soul prepares us to die.

If the ultimate purpose of human life is to become attuned to this greater state we are speaking about, then of course every discipline in one way or another has to contribute to that.
—Jacob Needleman

And the end of all our exploring will be to arrive where we started and know the place for the first time.
—T. S. Eliot

6

Loving Relationships

> *It has often been noted that most, if not all problems brought to therapists are issues of love. It makes sense that the cure is also love.*
>
> —Thomas Moore

> *Soulful love takes many forms...at its most basic, Eros is the drive in all things to complete themselves. This life force is the soul that makes flowers blossom and acorns become oaks.*
>
> —John Bradshaw

Human interactions or relationships are equally important at every stage of growth and development, and they undergo many transitions throughout a lifetime. Our loving relationships are those which enrich our lives and bring us our greatest pleasures; paradoxically, they also can bring us great sadness. As we move forward in exploring the loss and grief of living, it is necessary that we look at family systems, marriage, and divorce at a psychosocial-spiritual level.

I feel that most contemporary therapies fall short in their attempt to heal our emotional pain and suffering in intimate relationships because they have neglected the wisdom and resiliency of the soul as it relates to matters of the heart.[1] However, our living actions and behaviors are guided by our conscious mind and/or unconscious elements of which we are unaware. We must raise our awareness to include the polarities inherent in the human soul. Remembering that the study of psychology is both a science and an art, we can look to the creative artistry of the soul to assist us in healing our relationships. The language of the soul is symbolized and expressed through the musical and poetic rhythms of emotions. The continuum of emotionality ranges from fear to love, with a myriad of conflicting feelings in between. Both these primary emotions and all the secondary feelings along the continuum choreograph what internationally acclaimed author and lecturer Harriet Goldhor Lerner described as the "dance of intimacy."[2]

Marriage and Family

We form relationships instinctively because we are, in part, social beings. It is our nature to bond with one another. We interact with each other at varying degrees and levels of love and intimacy. The parent-child bond is different than the spousal attachment. The relationship of siblings has different meaning than that which we share with friends. The intensity of each relationship is personal and therefore one is not of greater or lesser importance than the other. Each of us has the liberty to define and assign value to each of our relationships.

Some say the parent-child bond is the most intimate and therefore the loss of a child or parent is the greatest. Others say that a long-term spousal relationship has the greatest sense of attachment and it is this loss that creates the most pain and suffering. I have discovered there is no universal consensus and this is due to the fact that we all are unique individuals and have developed our own meanings and values, especially in regards to death. I find the age of the deceased and the age of the survivor(s) to be relevant.

One does not need to be a marriage and family counselor to recognize the emotional pain and suffering of divorce, the ending of a long-term relationship, and familial estrangement; multiple loss surrounds the issue of divorce and/or the dissolution of any meaningful relationship. These are the attachments of the living world which touch our hearts most intimately and therefore create the greatest degree of imbalance to the psyche. My heart aches each time I witness commercial abuse by those who capitalize on and perpetuate human pain and suffering. When one becomes attuned with his/her soul and honors the sacredness of humanity's suffering as a journey or transformation towards grace, then he/she would never contribute to, or participate in, this form of exploitation.

There is much evidence that children are the ones who suffer the greatest loss during divorce. The main reason for this truth is that they, the children, have no choice in the matter. In this regard, the loss is like death. When a couple decide to get a divorce, their children's sense of belonging and security disappear and their souls feel divided and splintered. Mental confusion, uncontrollable emotions, and a sense of disconnectedness invade their sense of safety, state of well-being, and spirit. Many children must go forward having lost a relationship with one parent, usually the father.

Recently, I have become aware that many of America's courts are giving joint custody of children to parents when they divorce. In most cases, this seems absurd when the child or children are young. Young developing children need security, consistency, continuity, a sense of home and belongingness, and one simple set of guidelines motivated by love. Most couples divorce because they cannot get along in the weakest of cases, and/or because there is some kind of abuse in the severest of instances. Why would the courts feel that just because a couple divorces, all of a sudden they will miraculously be able to raise children together in a peaceful and loving environment? I understand the position of dividing time so that both parents are responsible and continue to enjoy the privilege of their parental rights. But, how about the child or children's rights? Do they not have the right to a nurturing home and some sense of normalcy? Dragging baby bottles, favorite toys, and most important, the child from house to house every other week is NOT in the best interest of the child. Common sense tells us this will cause confusion to the developing mind and create many fragile psyches as these children grow. I am very concerned about what this is doing to the soul of American children.

My clients, my students, and my own children shared that their parents' divorce caused them the greatest psychological pain and suffering that they have ever experienced. In some respects, divorce is more damaging to the psyche than losing a parent to death.[3] Even children recognize that terminal illness and death are aspects of a larger reality over which we have little or no control. But to think that a parent chooses not to be a part of the family unit is incomprehensible to young children. Many children, depending on their age, blame themselves for this loss of family unity. This creates a sense of shame which is carried forward until their grief is resolved.

My daughters were supportive of my decision to leave their father because they knew it was the best thing for me. This created a dichotomy for them. On the one hand they recognized that their father and I had grown apart in separate irreconcilable ways. They knew we would be healthier and happier by dissolving our marital partnership. On the other hand, however, they were frightened as their sense of home, security, and safety were taken away from them. They endured a heavy sense of responsibility and guilt in this matter. My heart still aches as I think of the pain I have caused both my daughters.

As parents we do not realize the emotional hell we put our children through. My older daughter, who was twenty-one, said the divorce caused doubt, fear, low self-esteem, sadness, mental confusion, headaches, stomach problems, and a sense of loss concerning the family unit. Her grades plummeted as she couldn't concentrate due to her grief. It took several semesters to regain her mental clarity and recover her high academic standing.

My other daughter was only fifteen at the time her father and I divorced. Recently, she disclosed that at the time of the divorce and for several years afterward, she experienced a deep sense of loss and security for her home, friends, and neighborhood. Sadness and depression manifested with anger, not at her parents but at the situation. The holidays and special events are still hard to cope with and she often feels conflicted as to with whom she will spend these special occasions. She said, "It gets easier as I develop more of a relationship with Dad and his new wife." She also commented that the one positive thing that came from this experience was her first-person knowledge of how alcohol affects people's lives. "You could have warned us about the effects of drinking and it wouldn't have mattered; but to really live it is different. The experience of divorce caused by the disease of alcoholism has helped me to make better decisions now that I am in college."

My daughters' experiences in this matter are not unique. As my students share their experiences of parental divorce, I hear the same manifestation of loss and grief echoed over and over. However, we must remember the paradox. As I soulfully listen to my daughters and students, I also hear sentiments of acceptance, gratitude, happiness, and understanding, as well as the symptoms of much personal growth. In my family's experience, our collective exploration of my daughters feelings surrounding divorce was profoundly enlightening to all of us. Many children, regardless of their age, are actually glad that their parents divorce. Though they experience all of the above mentioned realities of loss and grief, at the same time they have positive feelings. Children sense both the joys and sadness of their parents' relationship.

Similarly, we find this in the area of death and dying. With terminal illness, we are grateful and happy that our loved one makes the transition to death because we no longer have to witness his/her suffering day after day. Likewise, divorce is the closure to parental fighting, arguing, and unhappiness. Children are relieved of being caught in their parents' war or abyss of pain and suffering. So we see the soul and all its raw material present in marriage, divorce, and death.

Many times we see loss and grief issues for children in families where both parents are physically present in the home. One or both parents may be emotionally and/or spiritually void in their interactions with each other, and therefore with their children. This creates a sense of abandonment and brings many of us into therapy years later. This psychic or emotional absenteeism by parents interfaces with the ego developmental stages of the child and is very damaging. Psychic loss is a far subtler deprivation than the physical loss of the parent.[4] We cannot consciously objectify this sense of loss, and therefore it is not adequately mourned and will have a pathogenic effect.

In their book, *The Problem of Loss and Mourning*, Dietrich and Shabad explain:

> *If one night, for example, a father sits quietly in his living room without speaking to his child, the child will most likely not be traumatized. However, if night after night, year after year, the child is ignored by that same father, a traumatic pattern may establish itself that then constitutes the basis of the psychic loss experience. The traumatic themes of a parent's exploitation of a child for narcissistic purposes, the withholding of love, harsh criticisms, moody silences, and excessive intrusiveness all may induce feelings of psychic loss to a greater or lesser degree. The omission and commission of little acts such as never being kissed goodnight, having small promises consistently broken, or*

79

*being called a stupid child, when repeated over a number of
years, may each develop into a traumatic theme.*[5]

This affects adults too. Even when children are grown and
married themselves when their parents divorce, they can feel
betrayed and angry about the fact that their family of origin has
been ripped apart. They display a sense of disbelief and shock
because they had idealized their parents' relationship, only to
be hit in the face with the fact that it may have been less than
perfect. This realization may be disruptive enough to splinter
their concept of self, and in turn cause spousal relationship is-
sues for them. Loss and grief issues, if not worked through, can
become multigenerational.

Turning our attention to the divorcing adults, we become
aware of a similar paradox. Divorce was my saving grace when
I felt I was drowning in quicksand. My husband and I were no
longer meant to be together. We were at a place of destruc-
tion, only hurting ourselves, each other, and our children. As
painful as the process of detachment (divorce) was, it was nec-
essary so that my present state of peace, joy, and happiness
could emerge. I pray that our divorce rewarded my husband
with similar blessings.

I cannot speak for my husband, but during our divorce and
for the following two years, I experienced every symptom of
grief imaginable. What a turbulent period! Mostly, I suffered
confusion, anger, emptiness, and a sense of unwholeness. I had
never really been alone in my life. Though my childhood was
full of grief, I always had the feeling of belonging to a big fam-
ily. Now I was alone and had no one to depend on. I was also
ashamed, embarrassed, and full of guilt for not being able to
hold my marriage together. I felt worthless, unloved, unappre-
ciated, stupid, fearful, unattractive, scared, and isolated as I with-
drew from the world. I became very depressed and through the
healing processes of psychotherapy, prayer, meditation, twelve-

step recovery programs, and reflection, I began to emerge from the darkness of divorce.

As I reintroduced myself to my soul and felt my deep sadness and darker aspects of the unconscious (especially my anger), I was renewed with peace of mind and a new outlook on life. Working through my grief of the divorce, I came to a place of acceptance concerning my early childhood. The family disease of alcoholism, present in my family of origin as well as my marriage, has been both a blessing and a curse. It is due to all the trauma in my life that I have come to have respect and reverence for the mystery and my part in it. Through the process of healing, my *daimon*—from Greek mythology referring to your spirit within—has emerged giving me hope, strength, courage, and the creativity to become my Holistic Self. As Nietzsche so wisely said, "That which does not destroy me makes me stronger."[6]

81

Responsibility and Realignment

Marriage and divorce are social constructs, the former being the birth of a union of two people and the latter the death or destruction of this sense of wholeness. Socially, we refer to marriage as an institution, and religiously we know it as a sacrament. Divorce is only a socially and culturally defended arrangement. I do not know of any religion that celebrates or sanctions divorce, but simply has been persuaded to recognize it.

It is due to the union of marriage that we learn from and are enriched by the presence of each other. Soulful love is about compromise or sacrifice and about gifts or rewards. It is about caring and sharing. It is about giving and receiving. It is about putting someone else first—putting the soul of the union before the individual ego. It seems to me that marriage has evolved to a place of being only about socioeconomic status with couple-ego as the driving force. Eros, the life force, is about the soul or spiritual energy that drives the couple to an interdependent state of beingness. We cannot love one another and be part of a sacred whole (marriage) unless we are first whole by ourselves and love ourselves.

Many men and women are afraid to commit themselves to an intimate relationship because they feel they are giving up a part of self to the mate or to the union. Historically, women have given up property and rights to their male counterparts, and men feel they have given up their freedom of promiscuity and carefreeness. Marriage has been an unegalitarian construct driven by the forces of cultural patriarchy and hierarchy. Divorce rates have been high during the twentieth century as the soul of humanity begins to balance out this unequal state. Hopefully, we are beginning to realign male and female energies to a place of harmony which allows each individual fulfillment of his or her own potential, while at the same time fulfilling the potential of their relationships or unions.

Once again, this is not about blame, but about responsibility. I did not know enough about mature love when I got married. Yes, I was capable of giving, and I did. I was overresponsible at putting my husband, the union, and my children first. I was underresponsible when it came to loving self and being able to receive love. This is what Harriet Lerner would call overfunctioning and underfunctioning in the mental process.[7] When I speak about loving self, it must be underscored that I am not referencing the ego. Love comes from the spirit, not the ego. Soulful love is about respect and reverence for the Holistic Self, which honors the Ultimate Spirit or God within and puts the soul of the union before the individual ego. Carl Jung adapted the principle of entropy, or the second law of thermodynamics, to describe this distribution of psychic energy. The soul is always trying to bring about balance of energies. Less ego energy results in more psychic energy to be used socially and spiritually. With conscious awareness of the balancing act of the soul, we can begin to function individually and collectively at a higher level.

I believe that marriage has been about couple-*ego* and should be more about couple-*soul* or spirit of the union. Mature love requires a redistribution of energy. We must move from ego to spirit, which we arrive at by listening, seeing, understanding, acting, and reacting from our hearts and soul instead of our egos. Due to this high-energy state of ego beingness, many of us go into marriage and relationships with the attitude, though it may be unconscious, of "what's in this for me?" We have a misguided sense of expectations. We look to our partners to make us happy and whole.

Each member of the relationship, male and female, has socialized ideals about the meanings and values of their role in the marriage. John Bradshaw, in his book *Creating Love*, calls for a demystification or a "waking up" to the facts about what love really means.[8] I interpret Bradshaw's wisdom to be a process of reevaluation for each of us as we let go of some of the images of love that we have fixed in our minds from our socialized past, and to open our hearts to the reality of love. What does love feel like, look like, smell like, and taste like? This is not a new idea. The ancient wisdom of Buddhism invites us to do this in all our affairs. The word Buddha means "Enlightened One" or "Awakened One." Integrated into Western ideology, this reality is about "Being Awake." Being awake or present in all our affairs, especially in human relationships, results in attention to the present reality, not our past memories or remembrances and our future dreams or expectations. As we strive to live in a Buddha state concerning our relationships, we will find consciousness of balance with love, compassion, and understanding.

As he references the work of noted family therapist Virginia Satir, who outlines the five freedoms of highly functioning people, John Bradshaw shares with us:

> *Demystification is about coming out of the isolation of our self-to-self trance and owning these five freedoms. We*

83

*see and hear what we see and hear rather than creating
positive and negative hallucinations based on what is safe
to see and hear. We think what we think rather than stay-
ing confused or thinking what we are supposed to think.
We feel our own feelings rather than numbing out or
taking care of someone else's feelings. We want what we
want rather than what they say we should want. And we
imagine our own possibilities rather than always play-
ing out our rigid role.*⁹

If we go into a relationship not being whole and yearning for
our mate to fill our emptiness, then we risk a high sense of loss
when we lose our connectedness to our partner. We do not have
to be married to experience these manifestations of grief as we
separate from lovers, significant others, family members, and
dear friends. From the exploration of teenage dating to the re-
discovery of companionship in later years, love and intimacy
are a natural and beautiful part of the human experience. Any-
time we have a meaningful, heartfelt relationship with another,
we invest our heart and soul; therefore, emotional suffering pre-
vails when we lose our connection to this sense of wholeness.
Or, we may go into a relationship feeling whole, but due to
energy imbalance, lose ourselves in the presence of the union.
The euphoria that goes with being in love often causes our psy-
chic energy to go spinning out of control.

The difference is that we won't feel that life is not worth liv-
ing and/or we can't go on because we lost our sense of self. When
we only identify our self-worth as wife, mother, sister, daughter,
or friend, then when we lose this relationship role, we cannot
recover a healthy self-identity and we get stuck or remain in a
state of abnormal or unresolved grief. If we are living in the
present as a whole self, our relationships are enhancements of
our sense of self; then, if we lose someone, our psychic or soul-
ful energies more easily realign themselves with renewed inter-

est and ability to form other relationships. Yes, we will still go through grief upon losing a partner to death or divorce, but we will more easily find our divine source of strength and courage to realign our psyche, moving through our grief.

So it depends on our psychological and spiritual sense of wholeness whether we look at death, divorce, and lost relationships as the end of the world or as an opportunity for growth and rebirth. All our human interactions and relationships are blessings from the other world. It is our choice and responsibility to honor them and keep them sacred. We each have many relationships that have varying levels and degrees of meaning and importance. By ministering to and cultivating the soul, we become more mindful of how to emotionally interact with each other. The soul is always available to unlock the mystery of our discontent and renew us with hope, gratitude, and the insight that enables us to go forward with living.

The soul knows both the pain and suffering and the joy and harmony of human relationships. It recognizes the darker side of the human world and helps us to balance this reality with the peace and ecstasy of the spiritual world. This is what the human journey is about: a mystery guided by both seen and unseen forces. Our challenge lies in what we choose to do with this reality. It is not about our losses and our rewards—it is about what we choose to do with them.

I believe if we put soulful emotion back into our relationships, we will not only have a deeper understanding of our differences, but we will be graced with respecting each other for our individual uniqueness and become more patient with and tolerant, accepting, and forgiving of one another. This attitude affects our behaviors and strengthens the family's sense of one...ness. This does not mean we put up with emotional, sexual, and/or physical abuse. Violence and abuse of any nature are not about love. They are about a splintered psyche, a loathing for self on the part of the abuser, which gets displaced on the partner or the family members. It is about the need to victimize, to hold power and control over another to feed the narcissism of the perpetrator.

Many children report that they join gangs to find a sense of family, acceptance, love, and belongingness. What else can we expect if parents and adults in the community of humanity cannot provide and fulfill this need for them? We must take immediate steps to stop the wars in America's families and homes if we are to alleviate the wars between our children. We must learn how to deal with our emotional pain and suffering and open our hearts to the soul of life.

> *All intimate relationships require some degree of magic, because magic, not reason and will, accomplishes what the soul needs.*
>
> —*Thomas Moore*

> *Relationship is not a project, it is a grace.... Responding to the grace of relationship, it is important to appreciate, to give thanks, to honor, to celebrate, to tend, and to observe.*
>
> —*Thomas Moore*

7

All God's Children
(Life's Extraordinary Conditions)

> *Awareness of my pain keeps me aware of*
> *their pain, keeps my heart open to*
> *suffering.*
> —Treya Killam Wilber

> *Your body is the harp of your soul, and*
> *it is yours to bring forth sweet music from*
> *it or confused sounds.*
> —Kahlil Gibran

Rumi, the ancient Sufi poet, said, "You are the unconditional spirit trapped in conditions."[1] The conditions of the material world present us with many physical, mental, and emotional challenges. We can perceive these challenges as obstacles to our freedom, keeping us prisoners of fear, or as opportunities to develop our fullest living potential. I offer this chapter in the spirit of education as many of us live with special conditions that create extended periods of stress and anxiety for not only the individuals who suffer with the mental, physical, or emotional dis…ease, but also for their loved ones as they travel this human journey together.

I believe that within each of us there is a divine essence, a creative source that helps to heal any disenfranchised parts of the

Holistic Self.[2] Some of us may be born with physical or mental conditions that hinder functioning at the same level or degree that others in our society are privileged to enjoy. Historically, this population has been shunned and labeled abnormal, handicapped, or disabled. The more contemporary terms are people with physical or mental challenges or persons with special needs. I applaud this new terminology as it reflects a more compassionate society. The fact is that we are human beings and therefore all of us are disabled or dysfunctional to one degree or another.[3] Also, each of us has special gifts and talents to offer that are unique. So the level or degree to which we are able to live with dignity and purpose depends on the degree to which our culture or peers accept us with all our weaknesses and our strengths.

This is a complex and multifaceted area of loss and grief. Certainly we recognize that some conditions are much harder to overcome or cope with than others. These conditions may range from diminished structural and/or functional qualities at birth, such as mental and physical disabilities, to terminal illness and the waning characteristics of old age. This can manifest in one, several, or all parts of the Holistic Self. These challenges can be of the mind, body, soul, or spirit of the individual.

Keeping in mind my holistic paradigm, I acknowledge that these parts of self are interrelated and affect each other. I cannot tend to all the possibilities of special needs that are present in our society, as they are too large in number and individual in meaning. Instead, I will address those needs that I have personal experience with or knowledge of, those which I feel touch or affect our national community to the greatest degree.

Physical Challenges

I came into this world whole of body. Except for genetic predispositions to various conditions, I was fortunate to arrive with complete and healthy body parts. But there are thousands of individuals who are born each year with special circumstances. If we are born with underdeveloped or missing parts of our physical body, we have a difficult time fitting into our society because culturally the "populace norm" is not equipped physically, emotionally, or spiritually to embrace us. Physically, public arenas are designed for the majority rule or to satisfy what is needed to accommodate the average person. In recent decades we have made important strides in meeting the needs of the physically less fortunate. However, there is still more education and advocacy needed in cultivating the awareness of the emotional and spiritual aspects of those who suffer with physical limitations.

My personal journey as a person with physical limitations began in middle age. At the age of forty-two, I broke three cervical vertebrae in an auto accident. They were severe fractures, and the repairing procedures and ongoing healing process did and still do require more energy than I knew was possible to have. My loss goes far beyond structural damage. I lost range of motion, endurance capacity, and the ability to move or maintain a number of postural positions. Those of us who suffer with missing or limited body parts experience living in a world that is hard to explain.

89

We must be creative in learning to function in different ways. This is a long and arduous process and unique for each individual. It requires faith, courage, imagination, strength, determination, and persistence. Also, and most important, it requires a support person or group, such as family, who travels this journey with us. Our loved ones go through a sense of loss and grief that, though different, is sometimes equal to ours. Without the love, support, patience, and understanding of the people we love and live with, those of us who are physically challenged cannot overcome our limitations.

This brings me to another sense of loss, the loss of independence. The physically challenged are dependent on others for assistance, as are the terminally ill. It is a humbling experience to reach out and ask for help. We must do this if we are to accept our condition and move forward to join the living. There are many who experience grief, which manifests in feelings of helplessness, anger, sadness, low self-esteem, and of being different and not fitting in. We go through bouts of depression, hopelessness, exhaustion, and loneliness. There are many periods of just simply wanting to give up. We feel we are a burden to our families and wonder what we did to deserve this hell. Thoughts of suicide are not an uncommon reality.

Also, we suffer a sense of loss of what could be. I feel that I am missing out on life because I cannot do certain things. I miss not being able to participate in sports and go dancing. With limited functional ability and a limited supply of energy, I know I will never be able to work a forty-hour week again. I worry about being able to support myself, as I am a single woman. This reality brings with it ongoing pressure and anxiety. I am not able to do ordinary housework and have had to learn to ask for help and let go of my "perfectionist" personality characteristic that always had to have a sparkling clean house. These lost experiences change our perceptions of our wholeness. We cannot do the things we used to do. We must grieve these losses and move forward.

So that we do not remain victims of our circumstances, it is imperative that we heal the psyche around the trauma of our condition and learn how to celebrate life. The soul is our saving grace. As it recognizes and allows us to express our pain and frustrations, it is also our gateway to exploring our divine essence or heart from which emerges a creative force bringing balance to the Holistic Self. The soul becomes our ally in restoring all our sense of loss.

Optimistically, we realize that humankind has always prevailed over its afflictions and maintain hope that we always will. An encouraging example of this is shared in Dietrich and Shabad's book *The Problem of Loss and Mourning*. It states:

90

With regard to bodily losses and their restorative-creative potential, a brief historical review may be useful. Hephaestus, the god of art and artisanship (there was no sharp differences between the two in those days), was lame. His masterwork, according to Homer, was the Shield of Achilles, replete with depictions of figures dancing, running, fighting—all of them in active and impressive motion. Among all the gods on Mount Olympus the "renowned lame god," as Homer calls him, was the one who understood, promoted, and created art. Homer himself, according to tradition, was blind. Socrates, the great philosopher of antiquity, was physically misshapen, had a bulbous nose, and was otherwise unattractive in physical appearance. To go still further back, Moses, the most prominent figure of the Old Testament and founder of the Hebrew religion, was <u>aral sefoyajim</u>, as the scriptural text has it; that is, he suffered from a speech defect of such intensity that his brother Aaron had to serve as his mouthpiece for his talks with Pharaoh, to "let my people go."[4]

Several years ago I watched two interviews with Christopher Reeve, an actor who portrayed Superman on the big screen. Now a quadriplegic due to a horse-riding accident, he is a spokesperson on the president's council for research assisting all Americans who live in this physical stillness. The tears streamed down my face as I listened to the hope, strength, and courage he offered all of us who suffer with spinal cord injuries. I think of him and his burden, which is so much heavier than mine, every time I feel like giving up. His faith in God and trust in medical science, which he believes will help him to walk again some day, renews and fuels my heart and soul. His consciousness and spirit are overwhelmingly present as he celebrates life with the highest sense of dignity I have ever witnessed. He is a living exemplar for all humanity and truly a Super Man.

My reality of living with physical pain is shared by many people, an experience I wish no one would have to know. It is an ongoing reality of testing one's resolve to maintain some sense of integrity. All human beings, at one time or another, suffer and endure physical pain—be it with childbirth, a headache, a toothache, etc. Those of us who live with acute, chronic pain from spinal cord injuries, migraines, complications of cancer and AIDS, degenerative bone and muscle diseases, and arthritis know a degree of human suffering that goes beyond the definition of physical pain. Living in pain, day after day, month after month, and year after year, drains our energy and wears down our defense mechanisms.

Personally, I have used pain medications, ice/heat packs, isometrics, somatic exercises and bio-feedback, massage and physical therapy, deep breathing and relaxation techniques, pressure-point injection therapy, acupuncture, meditation, and prayer. All these things help to ease the pain; but, the reality is, to live life, to participate in and contribute to life, I do so always accompanied by a certain amount of pain. To some degree, I believe in mind over matter, so I blamed myself for not being enlightened enough to transcend my physical pain. Most recently, I have come to know that by accepting my condition, embracing my pain, and honoring it as a reminder to "heal thyself," my burden is lighter and I have more compassion for others. I live my life with purpose knowing that I must have reverence for the mystery and surrender to my human weaknesses while participating with my strengths. This balance enables me to walk forward as I assist others. Reading Jeffrey Mishlove's *Thinking Allowed* interview with Stephen Levine helped me to see my condition in a different light. I pass Levine's wisdom on to you.

> *You are not responsible for your illness....You are responsible to your illness.... In fact, even many meditative techniques for working with pain are to take your awareness,*

> *your attention, and put it elsewhere. Just when that throb-*
> *bing toe is most calling out for mercy, for kindness, for em-*
> *brace, for softness, it is least available. In some ways it is*
> *amazing that anybody heals, considering our condition-*
> *ing to send hatred into our pain, which is the antithesis of*
> *healing...our sense is that when you touch that which is in*
> *pain with mercy and awareness, there is healing; where there*
> *is awareness, there is healing.... To heal is to become whole,*
> *to come back to some balance.*[5]

As Treya Killam Wilber shared her journey of living with can-
cer in *Grace and Grit*, she acknowledged, "Awareness of my pain
keeps me aware of their pain, keeps my heart open to suffer-
ing."[6] She is referencing the pain of other cancer patients with
whom she worked diligently and to whom she ministered un-
failingly. Her ability to live with courage and dignity has been a
shining light for me. Though she has transcended her pain and
flown with the wind to the other world, she remains in spirit an
angelic example to all of us who suffer with physical diseases or
bodily impairments.

We must have special reverence for those who suffer with
more than one physical challenge. Before dying at the age of
sixty-seven, my dear friend and mentor, Margaret, lived with
diabetes. She developed Type I insulin-dependant diabetes at
the age of forty-eight after her son committed suicide. Usually
this type of diabetes is developed in adolescence. She believed
that this traumatic event in her life was directly responsible for
her condition. It was her body's way of responding to the death
of her only son.

As the disease took its toll on her mind, body, and spirit, she
wrestled with her soul to find peace and acceptance. Several
years before she died, she lost most of her vision and was unable
to read her blood-sugar test. Her ankle bones had crumbled and
she wore a leg brace, allowing her to walk. She suffered with

poor blood circulation in her extremities as do many diabetics. The last year of her life she lost kidney function and depended on dialysis three times a week, three to four hours at a time, to live. Her journey of living with this debilitating disease created many losses and much grief for her and her family. However, her presence, the beauty of her essence and her wisdom, which she offered everyone with whom she came in contact, was a sacred gift that I felt privileged to receive. Her courage, resiliency of spirit, love and understanding of the human experience, and respect for the Divine Mystery guided her through each day and was a blessing for me.

Margaret and others who suffer multiple physical traumas, such as those who live with HIV/AIDS, are our teachers and guides. They teach us, the ordinary people, how to live life with dignity, how to cultivate respect for humanity and all its absurdity, and how to endure suffering and to celebrate life. They know that the human experience is about love and compassion. They witness living in both worlds—the spiritual and the physical, the sacred and the profane. I thank God for their presence in our lives.

94

Mental Illness

The *Diagnostic Statistical Manual of Mental Disorders* (DSM) is a reference guide for mental health professionals. It categorizes a host of symptoms and enables psychiatrists and psychologists to treat those who suffer with mental illness. Mental illness is defined in Arthur S. Reber's *Dictionary of Psychology* as "a psychological or behavioral abnormality of sufficient severity that psychiatric intervention is warranted.... With implicit assumption that this disability is caused by some psychic 'germ' in a fashion analogous to the manner in which a somatic illness is caused by some biological infestation."[7] The medical model uses the term "mental disease" to describe abnormal behavior. A more neutral term is "mental disorder." Most of us realize that this complex issue under discussion has somatic (of the living body), genetic, biochemical, neurological, emotional, and, I believe, spiritual components. Whether one uses the DSM or the *International Classification of Diseases* (ICD), which in some cases are markedly different, we are classifying certain human beings as being different from the norm—if for no other reason than to accommodate the insurance companies.

The very first paragraph in Ronald J. Comer's *Abnormal Psychology* textbook gives us a clear picture of who is likely to have mental illness. He states:

> *Mental dysfunctioning crosses all boundaries—cultural, economic, emotional, and intellectual. It affects the famous and the obscure, the rich and the poor, the upright and the perverse. Politicians, actors, writers, and other public icons of the present and the past have struggled with mental dysfunctioning. It can bring great suffering, but it can also be the source of inspiration and energy.*[8]

95

This suggests to me that mental illness can strike anyone. Many of us who suffer or have suffered as "unconditional spirits trapped in conditions" have as much trouble defining our situation as do the experts. There are many explanations for abnormal and normal behavior. Today, we recognize mental illness as being both somatogenic (physical or biological) and psychogenic (of the psyche or soul) in nature, with socioeconomic and spiritual contributing factors. Noted psychiatrist, author, and lecturer M. Scott Peck contends that "Conditions like schizophrenia are not just somatic disorders....Virtually all disorders are not only psychosomatic but psychospiritual-socio-somatic."[9] I couldn't agree more, as through my personal experiences and observations I am witness to this holistic approach offered by Peck.

Sometimes I feel it is damaging to label individuals, as it creates harmful stereotypes and can affect one's sense of self. However, I also recognize the importance of identifying the elephant that may be standing in the living room. Several friends have told me they felt a huge sense of relief when they finally had a name for the chaos they were living with when their children were diagnosed with mental illness. These mothers were at their wits' end after years of coping with and trying to raise these special children who were different from their siblings.

Personally, I remember the shame of being different and unable to identify why. The elephant present in my home was my father's disease of alcoholism, which in the 1950s was not recognized as mental illness. Even if it had been, I don't know that my life would have been any different for two reasons: (1) in that decade we put the insane or mentally ill in asylums and institutions instead of outpatient treatment programs with family education and counseling; and, (2) this disease is often associated with denial, which shrouded my family in a heavy sense of guilt, shame, and fear. We became its prisoner, void of any emotional response or clarity of mind, so I feel certain my father wouldn't have been institutionalized anyway. The social repercussions of admitting to being an alcoholic or having an addict in one's family were devastating. Before the disease paradigm emerged in regards to drug and alcohol abuse, the individual and his/her family were castigated and judged as moral deviants.

The spousal abuse that was perpetrated by my father was also an area of shame and disgrace and went unacknowledged. It took me many years to deal with these horrific memories. Ronald and Patricia Potter-Efron wrote a book entitled *Anger, Alcohol, and Addiction*, which I recommend to you. They state, "A history of physical or sexual abuse has often been linked with alcohol and drug problems," and "Alcohol and drug use have often been associated with child abuse, sexual abuse, and spousal abuse."[10] Society is finally taking a hard look at all these issues and I pray that we will continue to assist those who still suffer in silence.

Part of my healing process was to deal with my anger at both my father and my ex-husband. Before I could be angry at the disease, I also recognized that I was angry at myself and at God— angry for allowing the addict and the disease to control my life. One of the reasons that I drank addictively for ten years was to keep my feelings suppressed. Drinking calmed my frustrations and allowed me to deny that I was suffering the loss of my mother, unresolved issues of fear, the loss of my childhood, and the victimization of rape. When we abuse drugs in this way, what we are really doing is numbing our pain. But what happens is, once we cross that line where the alcohol controls us instead of us controlling our lives, we either turn the pain inward on self, verbally lash out at others, or physically lose control. Thank God I didn't resort to physical violence as my father had. Unconsciously, I chose to turn inward on self, causing physical, mental, emotional, and spiritual dis...ease to my Holistic Self. Occasionally, I raged inappropriately, like a pressure cooker that had to release some energy or explode. My emotional, physical, and mental health were slowly deteriorating as my soul took up residency in the abyss of darkness.

This kind of mental illness (drug and alcohol addiction) has profound effects on all our behaviors, attitudes, and beliefs; it ripples out and touches all aspects of our lives. We lose our sense of reality, self-respect, self-esteem, and connection to spirit, living on an emotional roller coaster with no consciousness of our distorted or delusional thinking. In my Sonoma State University graduate research, I found that the manifestations of loss and grief, which correlate with drug and alcohol abuse, are anger, guilt, denial, and a sense of hopelessness.[11] These significantly paralleled those of loss due to the death of a loved one. These psychological, mental, physical, and spiritual symptoms are true for both the addict and his/her family. I don't know which was more painful, being the alcoholic or the daughter of the alcoholic. I am witness to both and cannot separate the two identities. All of this because I never learned to deal with my emotions and feelings; all of this because I never grieved my losses.

Twelve-step recovery programs, based on the earliest and most successful model of Alcoholic Anonymous, are spiritual avenues of healing for those who suffer with chemical dependencies and/or substance abuse disorders, and for their families as well. The first step on the road to recovery is breaking down denial, admitting we are powerless over our addiction or that a loved one is addicted and we are powerless to change them. But, we *can* do something. I have learned that the best thing we can do for our family member or friend who is the addict is to support their process while at the same time setting our boundaries and limits. Maturing and transforming one's self is not easy, and we must remember that we can only change ourselves—the addict has to learn to change him- or herself. It is about acknowledging that there is an elephant in the living room and seeing it for what it really is. One of the most important tenets of this philosophy is facing the reality that our healing is an ongoing life process.

It is no coincidence that these tenets parallel the first and last stages of the dying process put forth by Elisabeth Kubler-Ross, as this classification of emotional illness is a psychological death of the spirit within. As one wants to deny the reality that he/she is dying or that a loved one has died, one also wants to deny the reality of his/her own addiction. Coming out of denial gives us the opportunity to heal. Acceptance of one's condition, be it mental or physical illness, one's own impending death or losing a loved on to death is crucial. Acceptance is about being aware or mindful of one's reality—accepting the polarities of the soul. Acceptance is in fact letting go. Through this process, acceptance becomes a form of grace, receiving the spirit or our sense of unity consciousness back into our awareness.

Another form of mental illness that is overwhelmingly present in today's society is posttraumatic stress disorder (PTSD). Like all mental illness, its diagnostic criteria are complex and range from mild to severe. Historically, the most referenced cases are prisoners of war, war veterans, and holocaust survivors. Their pain and suffering has taught humanity a great deal about trauma due to research in this area.

The current Zeitgeist acknowledges experiencing PTSD resulting from more individual situations. I mention prolonged trauma because I have personally experienced posttraumatic stress due to my auto accident and as a survivor of rape. Increasingly, we witness PTSD as it correlates to the lifelong process of grief around incest and sexual abuse which seems to be rampant in this country. Ongoing denial of this reality causes many Americans, usually women, to suffer in silence. In their book, *Treating the Adult Survivor of Childhood Sexual Abuse*, Jody Messler Davies and Mary Gail Frawley communicate:

> *Now, thanks to the pioneering efforts of such epidemiologists as David Finkelhor (1984), Diana Russell (1986), and Gail Wyatt (1985), we know that approximately one-third of all women are sexually abused before the age of 18. Of these, about 43% have been incestuously abused before they turned 18 years old. These numbers mean that over 20 million American females have a sexually abusive experience before adulthood, often at the hands of a loved and trusted relative.*[12]

Usually the victims are women, but more recently we are hearing emerging testimonies by men who are beginning to acknowledge their victimization. Leonard Shengold, a contemporary classical psychoanalyst, employs the term "soul murder" to describe the phenomenological experience of recurrent abuse and deprivation of incest survivors.[13]

My friend Janice, who is an incest survivor, shared with me her reality of mental dissociation, depression, sense of hopelessness and isolation, anger/rage, sadness, sense of never fitting in or belonging, and her ongoing judgmental negative stream of consciousness that persecutes her for all her behavior and actions. She suffered in silence because she had been threatened by her perpetrators and was afraid she would die. The darker side of her soul caused her to act out inappropriately throughout her adolescence: lying, stealing, abusing drugs and alcohol, skipping school, engaging in sexual promiscuity, contemplating suicide, and suffering from a distorted body image. Janice reports that for thirty years she spent a great deal of energy trying to preserve an idealized family image, as it was the only way she could identify herself as being real and okay. In *The Hidden Legacy*, Barbara Hamilton acknowledges that "the emotional essence of incest is to feel oneself becoming spoiled to the core and powerless to stop it."[14]

For the past eight years Janice has been on a conscious journey of healing the pain and suffering of her abuse as she finds herself a single parent of three, a college graduate, and a successful computer-software manager. She said to me, "I now know it is better to be the victim/survivor than to be the abuser or perpetrator. If I would ever have caused this much pain and suffering to any living thing, I could not live with myself." Her statement allows us to see her compassion and understanding for the mental-spiritual illness in her family. She has my utmost respect as she walks in the newly discovered light of her spirit while her soul helps her to discover balance and peace.

Posttraumatic stress disorder has many different causes with varying degrees of trauma and grief, depending on the severity of the situation and the length of time one must endure it. I suffered a milder degree of PTSD due to my childhood abuse and my auto accident. Emotional, mental, and spiritual disturbances to the Holistic Self may require a lifetime of healing. Before I move into more discussion about the life experiences of loss, trauma, and grief, it is important that I speak to the pain and suffering of the parents, siblings, and loved ones who share the living journey of the physically and mentally challenged.

Each time a new life is brought into the world, parents are usually filled with hopes, dreams, and expectations for their offspring. As noted by Ziolko in her chapter on "Counseling Parents of Children With Disabilities" excerpted from M. Nagler's *Perspectives on Disability*, there are similarities between a parent's process of accepting a child's disability and the attitudes toward death and dying explained in the stages reported by Kubler-Ross. Using this model, Ziolko describes the grieving process for parents of disabled children and labels the stages as (1) withdrawal or rejection, (2) denial, (3) fear and frustration, and (4) adjustment period.[15] Again we need to work through our feelings so we can come to a place of acceptance.

Parents of physically and mentally challenged children live a reality of ongoing stress, anxiety, and grief. If the child's condition is severe, parents may experience anticipatory grief as they await the pending death of their offspring. If the child's condition isn't terminal, then the parents will spend the rest of their lives ministering to the needs of these special children. The patience, devotion, inexhaustible energy, and unconditional love they muster is greater than that which any of us with healthy children can imagine. As an observer and witness, I have learned from my friends who live with these special circumstances that our society falls short in assistance and resources which could lighten their load.

Dealing with doctors, hospitals, proper diagnoses, medications, therapies, and insurance companies more often than not is a nightmare. Sleep deprivation, juggling work schedules, an inability to maintain some sense of familial and social attachments, and a lack of time and energy for other siblings and self

101

are all components of their daily lives. Sometimes this stress and anxiety goes on for years. They face an ongoing reality of frustration, sadness, confusion, disappointment, fear, denial, sense of helplessness and hopelessness, exhaustion and sometimes anger and depression. One friend who has a fifteen-year-old daughter with mental illness keeps telling me that all she needs is some respite and understanding from her community. Most of her pain and suffering is really caused by a culture with no heart and soul, no compassion and love. This is a good example of *ongoing or prolonged* grief. My mission remains one of education so we can begin to heal the soul of humanity.

I believe that physical and mental illnesses are not abnormalities of the human experience but conditions of the human spirit as it resides in the material realm of living. Sometimes this requires that we let go of futuristic dreams and accept the conditions of the present. It is through this process that we discover our sacred self which graces us with the wisdom, strength, and courage to celebrate life with all its sense of unfairness.

This chapter has been difficult to write for several reasons: revisiting the abuse of my past, sharing my pain in the present, and relaying the experiences of my dear friends. We suffer and rejoice each day as we all find the strength, hope, and courage to live the mystery. This has been both a grieving and healing process for me. My grief remains a frustration for the lack or absence of awareness, understanding, love, and compassion that is apparent in our society. I hope this disclosure will help my reader to understand my ministry of tending to the *heart and soul* of emotionality and cultivating the mind of human potential.

> *God grant me the serenity*
> *to accept the things I cannot change,*
> *courage to change the things I can,*
> *and wisdom to know the difference.*
> —*Alcoholics Anonymous*

8

Other Living Losses

> *A person who is beginning to sense the*
> *suffering of life is, at the same time,*
> *beginning to awaken to deeper realities,*
> *truer realities.*
>
> —Ken Wilber

> *We could bear any burden if we thought*
> *there was a meaning to what we were*
> *doing.*
>
> —Harold S. Kushner

Loss is about change, expected or unexpected. In the last few chapters we discovered that loss, change, and growth are present throughout our life span. Also, we explored the anxiety of separation due to divorce/relationship issues and the ongoing grief experienced by those who are physically and mentally challenged. However, there are many issues of loss and grief that are not as widespread, some receiving lots of attention while others seem to go unnoticed. This chapter attends to some obvious issues of loss and grief that are not necessarily universal, but nonetheless important.

The truth is that each experience of the human journey is significant, and with varying degrees of loss/grief there follows an expansion of awareness and a renewal of spirit. The more we let go of the socialized ego-self, the closer we become to the

soul and spiritual-self. This is the essence of the human experi-
ence, a process of being or becoming—becoming one with unity
consciousness. We cannot experience being or becoming with-
out the inevitability of change, remembering that with all change
comes endings and beginnings. Bringing a sense of closure or
acceptance to all the yesterdays and opening the doors to today
and tomorrow—this is true healing—peeling back the layers of
understanding.

Loss by Violence

Loss caused by violence includes rape, incest, physical as-
sault, and murder. These are hardest to grieve and therefore take
the longest to heal. My heart aches each time I hear of children
killing children for reasons of instant gratification in one form
or another. Spousal and child abuse are a national disgrace. It
seems to me that we have become so desensitized to violence
that we accept it as a norm. Violence breeds violence; anger
breeds anger. We must learn to feel our feelings in a nonde-
structive way and work through our pain and frustration instead
of projecting or acting out on our fellow human beings.

Earlier in the book, I shared my personal experiences with
rape and living with a violent father who took my mother's life.
I also had a niece who died at age two and a half as the result of
child abuse. Her death almost tore my family into irreparable
pieces. This violent death happened fifteen years ago and to
date we still don't know who killed her. The district attorney
dropped the investigation, which created further grief. Murder
is the worst form of death for both the victim(s) and the survi-
vors. It is impossible to find meaning in such deviant behavior
and therefore very difficult to arrive at some sense of closure.

Though war involves murder, we collectively rationalize it so
that we feel its necessity, decorate its heroes, and celebrate its
memory. But for my mother, my niece, Polly Klass, Nicole Brown,

Ron Goldman, and the thousands of others whose lives have been taken by the darker side of humanity's soul, there are no national memorials honoring their lives—casualties of the wars that rage every day in American homes.

I know that the experts say we must come to a place of forgiveness and acceptance in order to heal. Those of us who share these experiences of violence know that this is not exactly true. "The violent end to our loved one's life, the suffering they might have endured, the life they were cheated out of, is not acceptable." This statement comes from the unpublished research paper of one of my students, Mary Farrow. Her awareness is validated by Janice Harris-Lord, author of *No Time for Good-byes*, who states, "The sudden, violent killing of someone loved is never acceptable."[1] Lord goes on to discuss that though we can never fully realize acceptance, we can come to a place of acknowledgement. Acknowledgement does give us the opportunity to face the reality of our loss and begin our journey of healing. This may be a different process for each of us due to our unique personality and the circumstances surrounding the violent death of our loved one.

Those of us who grieve the loss of a loved one to murder can go through a lifetime of psychological and emotional hell if we do not work very hard to move on. Not only is the murder a sudden shock, but we feel we should have done something to prevent it, especially when the murder is perpetrated by a family member, someone we know to be violent. I carried inappropriate guilt for twenty years after my mother died. I want everyone to understand that harboring guilt does no one any good. These evil acts of violence are not our fault. And we could not have prevented our loved one's death. For anyone who is still naive enough to think that a batterer will not murder—you are living in denial. They will kill and do kill every day in this country.

Mourners go through every emotion on the continuum. We feel deep love for our lost family member while at the same time experience hate for their assassin. These mixed emotions render us incapable of thinking clearly and hinder our ability to function normally. We must talk out our rage and anger, as these emotions are normal; but they must be released or they will destroy us. Our deep sadness takes us into the abyss of darkness until we resolve our grief. Honor these feelings and work through them so eventually you will be free of your pain. Then there will come a time to make a decision. Yes, we do have a choice. Are we going to let hate and anger destroy us? Or, do we <u>choose</u> light over darkness? We can choose to spend our energy on love, not anger.

There are other forms of victimization that are important to look at. Some result in death and some do not. Some are collective and others are individual experiences. Those that result in death have additional complications of grief. However, those from which we escape with our lives are still very traumatic. The difference is that in these cases the victim suffers the loss and grief wherein the former scenario, the family and friends become additional victims or survivors who must go through the grieving process. In either case, we are rendered helpless in the situation and PTSD may result to varying degrees. Examples of victimization, other than the ones we have already mentioned, would be akin to verbal and emotional abuse, robbery, stalking, kidnapping, drive-by shootings, the gang and drug wars, and terrorism.

It is imperative that I speak to a form of domestic abuse that is hard to detect and therefore goes unrecognized and untreated in our society. First, I must say that domestic violence is not just about wife or partner battering. *Domestic* includes children and/or parents. I am speaking directly to verbal and emotional abuse, as I am witness to it as a therapist and have several sisters who have experienced this evil form of "soul robbing." There are many women, and I imagine some men, suffering due to verbal and emotional abuse. The abuser usually has personality issues of power and control; he lies, turns every situation around to benefit himself, practices authoritarian child-rearing techniques, isolates his partner from family and friends, verbally degrades and finds fault with his spouse, displays passive-aggressive behavior, and drags his partner through an emotional hell that robs her of any sense of mental clarity, identity, self-esteem, or self-worth. Verbal and emotional abuse will often turn into physical violence. I cannot state strongly enough: "Abuse is Abuse!" This state of existence literally robs the victim of her soul. The victim suffers for many years until she removes herself from the abuse and begins to rebuild her sense of saneness and self-confidence. She needs our patience, understanding, and support as she rediscovers her soul which will help her to find peace.

Children suffer developmental losses and emotional grievances when they live in these emotionally and verbally abusive environments. Such homes are filled with drama and trauma, mental confusion and despair, with a sense of hopelessness that finally darkens the soul of both the mother and her children. I want to share some wisdom from one of my friends/colleagues with all women who are suffering in the darkness of these abusive relationships. She appropriately compares this sense of helplessness to the analogy of a passenger on a plane when an oxygen mask is required during flight. We are told to put the oxygen mask on ourselves first, which enables us to assist our children next. Mothers, we cannot save our children until we save ourselves first.

As of this writing one cannot escape the awareness of the terrorist activities that are happening in the Middle East. We do not have to look around the globe to appreciate the horror in this criminal behavior. Every country in the world, at one time or another, deals with the traumatic reality of terrorism. Not long ago, America had to deal with such trauma due to the Oklahoma City bombing; a few years earlier it was the New York Trade Center bombing. The senseless loss of life and the grief inherent in these devilish acts of terrorism go beyond the understanding of any of us who revere life as a sacred gift and part of the Divine mystery. We are left only with the position of trying to mend the hearts or minister to the souls of the traumatized and bereaved. As the nation came together, offering support and comfort to the families of Oklahoma City, and more recently to the communities directly involved in school shootings, I witnessed a wholeness or holiness that gives me hope for humanity. I cannot help but feel that if we offered this degree of kinship and love on a daily basis to our American brothers and sisters, these atrocities would not be taking place.

We must remember that all those who lost their loved ones or who were directly involved (including the rescue teams) in these darker hours of American history will need our love and support for many years. They have had their sense of safety stolen from them, their American rights egregiously violated, and their hearts and souls stricken with the deepest grief they have ever experienced. Many of us cannot go there to minister to the emotional aspects of their souls. But we can pray for them and send them our heartfelt love in a spiritual sense. The intentions of prayer and spiritual energy have a powerful mega-healing component which brings comfort, balance, and peace to both the receiver and the initiator. This is the law of Karma—if we project intentions of love and compassion towards others, we automatically receive it back into our lives.[2] It is a matter of energy exchange at the macrocosmic level of unity consciousness.

My daughter has given me permission to share one of her life experiences. Dawn moved to Washington, D.C., one year after graduating from college at the age of twenty-three. She had only lived there for three and a half months when she and her boyfriend, JT, were kidnapped, held at gunpoint, and robbed. The two young men who victimized them were after their ATM cards for cash. They drove Dawn and her boyfriend around in JT's car for several hours late one Friday night. This ordeal naturally traumatized both

Dawn and JT long after the young men returned them safely to their neighborhood. Their assailants were captured and brought to justice, which did offer some sense of relief.

However, it wasn't until two years later that Dawn began to feel safe again. As a mother I felt helpless, angry, sad, and frightened as I realized I could no longer protect my children from the world I had taught them to trust. I would like to share excerpts from the narrative which Dawn wrote as part of her healing process.

> *They told us they would shoot us...I ended up in the front passenger seat (specifically, sitting on the floor, face down on the seat). The first gunman was driving; JT was put on the back floorboards face-down, and the second gunman sat in the back holding his gun to JT. This is how we remained for the next hour-and-a-half...JT's legs had fallen asleep after about forty-five minutes, yet every time he tried to rearrange his legs the gun was thrust further into his back. I concentrated on memorizing the fabric pattern on the seat, while convincing myself that this was not the way I was meant to go. Not once were either of us close to tears. We somehow knew that unless we remained quiet, cooperative, and clear-minded, we might not come out alive. We became the perfect victims...The only goal in one's mind is that which exists to keep us alive...Since November of '93 I've told this story more times than I can count. Initially I told it as a means to heal. The more I shared my incident, the more I found others who had been victimized as well. Having others tell their stories, as well as how they had been able to move forward, helped a great deal...For at least two months, I carried thoughts of the incident with me daily, they had become a part of my identity. I was afraid to walk to and from the Metro station, for I had to walk past the street where we were abducted. I became very nervous at*

the thought of going out after dark. We avoided almost all social engagements in the evening for the two months that followed. I became angry that my freedom had been so casually taken from me. I asked myself "Why me?" and constantly looked for a reason that this should fit into the scheme of life. I strongly believe that everything happens for a reason. When I was unable to find a reason, it only made me feel helpless and vulnerable. After a few months we moved. Although I logically knew that I was no safer two miles outside the District, I was able to easily convince myself that I was. The psyche is interesting in that it allows one to create a false sense of security with only a slight alteration of the original situation...I have advanced to what seems like a new level of healing! I rarely think or talk about the incident. It is very seldom anymore that I go to bed afraid that someone will break into our apartment. And I have come to an understanding within myself about why this experience was a necessary part of my life. I began to think of the huge portion of the world's population that have had things much worse happen to them. I considered those who live in warring countries, or have fought in wars in the past. Children who barely survive day-to-day in third world countries, or refugees who risk their lives on poorly constructed rafts to cross the sea to a better future; these are the individuals I thought about to gain perspective on what had happened to me. I recognized that a necessary part of the human condition is having to feel the impact of traumatic experience; and that one grows and moves forward only by allowing these experiences to be building blocks to a better understanding of one's self. Although initially I was angry that this incident robbed me of my innocence and false sense of security, I am now able to view it in a very different light...I now look at my victimization as part of who I am; a part of me that is not negative or positive,

> but significant. I have gained a new confidence in myself with respect to adverse situations. I can now include "courageous" as part of my self. I realize that it wasn't my victimization that gave me courage, but rather that the experience allowed me to recognize that previously untested quality within myself.

When Dawn came to my grief class to share her story, hands went up all across the room. Dawn's courage in sharing her pain and suffering gave others permission to share theirs. It was a very healing afternoon for all of us.

Natural Disasters

Loss and grief occur with the presence and aftermath of Mother Nature at her most omnipotent display of power. Globally, it seems that in the past few years we have had a never-ending barrage of earthquakes, floods, hurricanes, tornadoes, and extreme hot and cold temperatures (possibly a result of global warming), which have had devastating effects on human beings. The effects of natural disasters traumatize individuals to varying degrees. Most noted are the cases of death and injuries to the physical bodies of our human species. When we look at loss in this area, we must also consider the other kinds of life that are destroyed. Floods and fires sweep away the landscape while deadening everything in their path, be it mineral or plant and animal life.

Many fires, which each year destroy thousands of acres of forest and all the sacred life within, are not always a consequence of nature but often created by the negligence of humankind. Fire in its very essence destroys the clean air we breath as well as other resources. The loss of clean air is apparent in the rising cases of upper respiratory infections and diseases. However, these conditions can also result from air pollution caused by urbanization and industrialization (used here in the broadest sense). Perhaps we should consider this the loss of our planet's soul in an ecological sense.

One of my students wrote a research paper on the loss of natural light in our night skies. Living in Los Angeles, he had to drive two hours from the city to see the stars and planets as he studied astronomy. He felt a sense of loss to artificial night light that radiates from every city. His sadness was in missing the relationship and the energy we receive from the heavenly grandeur of our cosmic neighbors.

The loss that affects us most directly from natural disasters is the loss of human life, injury to our physical body, and splintering of the psyche/soul. These types of loss are unexpected and usually multiple. The manifestations of grief begin with shock and numbness as we cannot believe it's happened to us, followed by fear, depression, sadness, sleeplessness, a sense of helplessness, anger, and mental confusion. Many people lose their homes and all their personal belongings, which results in the devastating reality of losing one's sense of security and sense of identity. We often identify ourselves with our environment and when this is abruptly taken from us, we become bewildered and unable to feel grounded and whole.

There is also the overwhelming financial stress of replacing everything. There are some things that we cannot put a price on for the insurance companies or that simply cannot be replaced: Grandmother's china, a child's favorite doll or stuffed animal, family pictures. Some people do not have insurance and thus become homeless. When we are unable to get our basic needs of shelter and food met, we are vulnerable to separation from Spirit. If a farmer's crops are destroyed by wind, hail, floods, etc., then he becomes financially bankrupt, losing his livelihood, possibly losing his trust and hope in his profession, which could ultimately lead to losing his sense of self. Our roles and professions identify us and give meaning and purpose to our lives. If we lose these identities, we feel like giving up.

Having completed a Critical Incident Stress Management Course, I have a profound sense of appreciation and awareness for the grief suffered by rescue teams. Our police officers, firefighters, paramedics and ambulance personnel, dispatchers, critical incident stress teams, chaplains, and others who risk their lives everyday to protect our citizenry see the darkest side of the soul of humanity. They need our help in adjusting to the death, senseless horror, and trauma they witness daily. We must offer them our compassion, love, understanding, and gratitude. This also brings to mind the emotional pressure, stress, and anxiety that emergency medical professionals go through—doctors and nurses. They deal with suicides, death, and terminal illness, and need to be educated as how to process and release the sense of loss and grief that they inevitably endure.

The personal trauma that results from natural disasters, though devastating to the psyche, seems to be a little easier for the intellect to handle than the earlier mentioned forms of victimization. As is true with death, terminal illness, or old age, we recognize that there is a higher, more powerful energy/force at work and we cannot do much but accept it, pick up the pieces, grieve our losses, and go forward. God against man, nature against man, these losses are orchestrated from the other world. Losses related to the wrath of nature are seen in a different light. These losses unite us as we come together to assist our neighbors with the healing process.

When the equation of *change + loss = growth experience* is caused by man against man, the mind has a more difficult time understanding—because it is about energy exchanges of this world. We suffer in silence and our friends and neighbors are not always there to support us. There is more shame and guilt with this kind of loss. We mortals attach a sense of judgement with the man-against-man losses, as if to say, "This would not have happened if you were a good person." I must emphasize that the intellectual mind needs to quit judging the emotional mind at both the individual and collective levels We must learn to listen with our heart

and soul, and perceive all emotional cues or warnings that some-
thing is out of balance. Only then can we grow to be a more
caring and compassionate humanity.

When we experience the pain and suffering created by man against
man, we know that it manifests from evilness of intentions executed
by fear, power, and greed—the darker side of humanity's soul. What
about the pain and suffering that does not stem from human inten-
tion? Is it a matter of entropy, of quantum physics, of randomness?
This question has plagued humankind since the beginning of time,
and except for some well-educated guesses, it remains the MYSTERY.
I do not have an answer for you. But, I do know that we are not being
punished and that we must not judge each other.

In ministering to human pain and suffering, I keep in mind
the wisdom offered by Harold S. Kushner in his best seller, *When
Bad Things Happen To Good People:*

114

> *Or it may be that God finished His work of creating eons
> ago, and left the rest to us. Residual chaos, chance and
> mischance, things happening for no reason, will continue
> to be with us, the kind of evil that Milton Steinberg has
> called "the still unremoved scaffolding of the edifice of God's
> creativity." In that case, we will simply have to learn to
> live with it, sustained and comforted by the knowledge that
> the earthquake and the accident, like the murder and the
> robbery, are not the will of God, but represent the aspect of
> reality which stands independent of His will, and which
> angers and saddens God even as it angers and saddens us.* [3]

Social and Cultural Loss

As I witness great numbers of Americans who are void of
emotion, calloused and insensitive of heart to violence, lack-
ing community consciousness, prejudiced to the point of think-

ing and acting as if they are better than others, I cannot help but know that we have lost the sacredness of the human spirit. I am deeply saddened. One way we feel connected to that which is larger than self is our sense of belonging to a neighborhood or community—our sense of being accepted and part of something. As mentioned in Chapter Six, disenfranchised kids joing gangs for this very reason. This is a scary reality, when our youngsters feel they must leave home and family to feel safe, wanted, and loved.

According to sociologists, urbanization has created some of this distancing. Ironically, the closer we live together, the farther apart we feel. We often see this in the adult population as well. We spend from nine to eighteen hours a day commuting and working, so it is natural that this environment begins to feel like family and home. It is our adult place of acceptance or unacceptance. It is our intellectual and social life—the place where many of us get our ego-strokes and sense of self-worth. 115

Corporate downsizing and economic movement into an international marketplace seem to be contributing to our sense of disconnectedness. Over the past several years we have heard of people losing their jobs and taking out their anger, depression, and sadness by machine-gunning their former place of employment. Some people are literally losing touch with reality, becoming psychotic and dangerous to self and others. Thank God these are rare occasions. I use this extreme example to make a point, that point being—when we lose our sense of identity, our means of livelihood or social/professional persona, we experience a profound sense of loss and grief. Grief, left unattended, has various repercussions of varying degrees. As companies lay off their employees or geographically relocate them, the employer must become sensitive to each person's ability or inability to handle change along with the stress that is created because of these changes. Common sense tells us that we are creatures of habit, and most of us feel safest and most secure in a known, comfortable environment.

When people geographically transfer or relocate, there is loss at both ends. We leave behind friends, family, and coworkers who will miss us, as we miss them. When I moved from Iowa to California at the age of nineteen, I went through a deep sadness. I left a small Midwestern farming community to live in a large seaboard city and the adjustments were overwhelming. My whole way of life was different. Change is not inherently good or bad—just different. This we need to recognize. I often think of those who leave their native land to live in a new country—what change, loss, grief, and growth they must experience. There is a delicate balancing act of retaining one's native language, customs, and rituals as one adapts to his/her new surroundings. America is a smorgasbord and therefore we must have reverence for our multiculturalism, our unique diversity. Whether we move from state to state or country to country, we all will experience loss and grief during the transition. I hope the time is coming where we embrace each other as ONE—celebrating our like...ness instead of agonizing over our different...ness.

Children are especially vulnerable to feeling loss when families relocate. They must leave their homes, teachers, and friends. When we are young, moving is more difficult because we are not conditioned to change, and adults often neglect to recognize that this profound sense of loss applies to children. In this culture we are notorious for trying to protect children by excluding them. We have come to recognize the healthiness of bringing children into the grieving process as it relates to death. We can apply this new awareness to the grief and stress of moving, as well as to the other areas of loss covered in this book.

Intimate Losses

I would like to bring awareness to some very personal and intimate losses, which are often well-kept secrets—kept secret because our culture has great fear and discomfort talking about sex and its related issues. There is often much psychological suffering around the realities of: abortions, miscarriages and/or still-births, breast reductions, sexual dysfunction, sterility, impotency, and adoption. When we do not recognize these psychosexual issues as loss, then we deny ourselves a healthy grieving process and find ourselves suffering emotionally in silence. Feelings inadvertently get repressed and can cause mental stress and other dysfunction. Any time one experiences a transformation in their physical, emotional, psychological, cognitive, social, and/ or spiritual process of growth, they go through a soulful death and renewal of psychic energy. Our human journey is an ongoing reality of life, death, and rebirth—a process of attaching, letting go, and transcendence.

We must remember that any change in our physical or spiritual self affects our social behavior. Women do not go through an abortion, miscarriage, or still-birth without a great deal of sadness. Also, feelings of inadequacy may emerge and depression may engulf us. When couples cannot conceive, they go through deep grief, sometimes for years. These lost opportunities of procreation affect both women and men. Historically and culturally, we have silently told women that if they cannot conceive and give birth, then they are "less than." Motherhood has been a female archetype for centuries. Hopefully, since the age of enlightenment and the women's movement, these ridiculous notions are on the decline. These losses affect our personality and therefore ripple out into all our relationships, attitudes, and behaviors. The sense of loss that accompanies these intimate experiences is normal and in order to heal we must recognize and work through our grief.

Breast reduction or loss of a breast to cancer can be both physically and psychologically painful. There are various health reasons why women choose breast reduction, but a certain degree of grief results as we are losing part of our bodies. I have heard this same grief in reference to a vasectomy and a hysterectomy.

These feelings are real and should be ministered to with loving care. When a female chooses or needs an abortion, or gives a baby up for adoption, there is a grief that only she understands. The women in America could work through these intimate issues of grief easier if the patriarchal establishment would keep their laws and judgements to themselves. These shame and fear tactics only cause more pain and suffering.

Sexual dysfunction and impotency create various emotions for both the individual who suffers, his/her spouse or partner, and their children. We can lose our sense of sexuality and our intimate attachment to others. We miss and long for the person we use to be. Depression, isolation, and anger often plague us. We must learn how to work through our sadness knowing that sexuality is akin to spirituality and we can be whole individuals. If we do not, all kinds of relationship issues and a misguided self will surface.

118

As for adoption, I will only say two things. First, we must be aware that not only is the mother, who gives her child away, in emotional pain, but the child suffers, too, in varying degrees depending on his/her new environment. This is a complex issue and must be sensitively ministered to, on behalf of both the mother and the child. Secondly, we must acknowledge that some of these adoptions are forced upon the birth mother, perhaps by parents who send their teenage daughter away secretly to give birth and relinquish her baby. I have wept for hours with women as they work through their personal sense of loss and intimate grief due to these special circumstances. If these cases involve rape or incest, additional trauma arises. In any of these situations, we should have reverent compassion.

I hope this section has illuminated an understanding that loss and grief are not just about death. Loss is inherent in all change and exchange of energy. Change is inevitable and the way in which we learn and evolve. Change is more easily accepted if we grieve what we have lost and celebrate the richness and new awareness of the experience. As we become more conscious of this reality, we will enjoy better physical, mental, spiritual, and psychological well-beingness. We will learn that being human is about the Both/And...ness of existence. We can learn to celebrate life as we minister to the needs of the soul. Working through the oscillating waves of human emotionality, we are actually healing the disenfranchised aspects of the soul.

In Section Three, I share insights that have been instrumental in my healing process. Concurring with my holistic perspective of mind-body-soul-spirit, I explain the psychosocial, physiological, and spiritual manifestations of grief; offer coping strategies; and discuss theoretical approaches to understanding the actualization of a more Holistic Self as we learn to accept life's challenges of separation and anxiety.

> *I recognize that a necessary part of the human condition is having to FEEL the impact of traumatic experiences; and that one grows and moves forward only by allowing these experiences to be building blocks to a better understanding of one's self.*
> —Dawn Marie

> *It has been said, and truly I think, that suffering is the first grace. In a special sense, suffering is almost a time of rejoicing, for it marks the birth of creative insight.*
> —Ken Wilber

Section Three

Healing: Ministering to the Soul

*You would know the secret of death, but
how shall you find it unless you seek it
in the heart of life.*

—Kahlil Gibran

9

Grieving is Healing

> Your pain is the breaking of the shell that
> encloses your understanding.
> —Kahlil Gibran

> In our attempt, as psychologists to
> eliminate suffering, we must observe what
> is being revealed in the suffering.
> —Thomas Moore

In Section Two we explored the separation and anxiety inherent in ordinary living. I have shown that loss is not only about the death of the physical body, but that we encounter a multitude of quasi-deaths or minipsychological deaths throughout the experience of being human. Aldous Huxley said, "Experience is not what happens to you; it is what you do with what happens to you."[1] Huxley's wisdom explains how I see the loss, separation, anxiety, and/or grief that comes with the journey of the human soul. How we react, neglect to react, or choose to act in regard to our pain and disappointments of the natural world is the degree to which we will suffer; hopefully, we emerge in joyous celebration of our human beingness.

How do we reeducate ourselves so that we honor humanity's suffering and at the same time receive the grace of joy that is available to each of us? Consider the perennial wisdom of Ram Dass, who shares that "suffering is grace," although he acknowledges, "I can't live it. I can live it at moments, with little sufferings; but I can understand that there is a beautiful unfolding of awareness through suffering."[2] I suggest that we live these moments of suffering by tending to the emotionality of the soul. As we rediscover our soul, we become attuned with the sacred self or the heart of our connection to the Divine Spirit. Using my metaphor of *Artichoke Heart*, we begin to understand that by peeling back the layers of psychological pain and suffering, we arrive at the heart of our true essence which offers us the freedom to become beings of what quantum physicist David Bohm would call *undivided wholeness* or what Danah Zohar refers to as *quantum self*.[3] One can also look at the artichoke leaves as being the many facets of the ego-personality that must go through the detachment process so as to become a disciple of the BOTH/AND concept creating an emergence with unity consciousness.

Evolution and socialization have embedded many ideas and concepts in our minds that need to be reevaluated, conscious reprogramming so to speak. I personally realized the "old tapes" from childhood were distorting my adult thinking and behavior. Being called a no-good-f——— whore by my father during adolescence left me with no love of self or sense of self-worth. Unconsciously, I carried this image around with me for forty years until I changed my thinking patterns. Awareness is the first step to change. Peeling back or separating the layers of mental confusion certainly was valuable in my healing process. New awareness, new definitions, and formulating new meanings—all of which are ongoing, lifelong processes— continue to bring forth enlightenment, hope, strength, and courage to move me through my pain and suffering. And, it is in between the breaths of crisis and anxiety that we learn to embrace and celebrate life.

Please remember that this is an ongoing process of "being" in the world. It is never over until death, at which time we transcend the conflicts of the soul as it rejoins the spirit of unity conscious-

123

ness. Our biggest responsibility is accepting this process of ministering to the soul as our greatest challenge. Remember that healing is not a cure but a ministry of reverence, tending to and caring for the emotionality of the soul. It is about creating balance between this world and the other world, detaching from the ego...ness of the physical and allowing an emergence of spirituality. After we have reached into the place of the heart, we know that it is an ever-fertile seed from which blossoms rebirth and new life—and then the process begins all over again.

My premise is that we must cultivate and minister to our emotions, as they are expressions of the soul. We must feel them, listen to them, taste them, and see them in all their complexity, and then make a conscious choice to extol them with the reverence of an alchemist—turning them over and over so as to examine every nuance—and through this creative process we will discover a state of beingness that rewards us with physical, psychological, mental, and spiritual health.

I cannot advise you individually how to do this, as it is a personal journey. But I can tell you I know that through your process of tending to the emotionality of your soul, and reaching into the depths of your heart, a creative force will emerge. Each of us can be a participant in creating our own joy if we have the courage to confront life's difficulties and the enthusiasm to emerge from our despair. From Jeffrey Mishlove's book *Thinking Allowed*, Joseph Campbell reminds us that the word *enthusiasm* means "filled with a god." So follow whatever makes you enthusiastic; be creative, be a creator of your higher self, and follow your bliss. "The bliss is the message of God to yourself. That is where your life is."[4]

The Spiral of Grief

The manifestation of loss and grief which I will be discussing are those that have been observed by hospice volunteers as they assist

Spiral of Grief™

Loss

Denial	Anger
Emotional Outburst	Guilt
Impeded Functioning	Restlessness
Sleep Disturbances	Impatience
Weight Loss or Gain	Ambiguities
Pain	Apathy
Hopelessness	Sadness
Depression	Mental Confusion
Helplessness	Anguish
Isolation	Fear
Loneliness	Low Self-Esteem
Abandonment	Loss of Interest
Sense of Release	New Interest and Skills
Renewed Energy	Renewed Sense of Self
Restored Mental Judgement	Courage and Strength
Understanding	Acceptance
Increased Awareness	Hope and Sense of Peace
Forgiveness	Love and Compassion

125

Peace

*Grieving is Healing
as Suffering is Grace*

bereaved individuals through the emotional turmoil of losing a loved one. My professional work with clients, my life experiences, and my study of the dualistic qualities of the soul, suggest that these psychological and physiological manifestations are congruent with the stress, anxiety, and trauma experienced during the many losses of living discussed in the last few chapters. These feelings or states of beingness are found along the continuum of emotionality that ranges from fear to love as expressions of the soul. The *Spiral of Grief* shows the range of emotionality that is the normal human response to loss and separation. Here is a list of the manifestations one may experience as a normal reaction to terminal illness, the loss of a loved one, and all the many challenges of change, separation, and grief/anxiety of the living world.

Guided by the wisdom of Kubler-Ross in her book *On Death and Dying*, we recognize that denial or disbelief of our situation is the beginning of our spiral into the abyss of psychological pain and suffering. This is the initial stage of "shock and numbness." The second phase is "searching and yearning" as we try to make sense of what has happened. This is usually followed by a period of "disorientation" as negative and positive energies clash with each other. We are presented with the choice between moving forward to find our bliss or remaining stuck in our pain. Finally, we come to the place of "reorganization"—which is a process of making choices and decisions and taking responsibility—and I promise you that it will come.

Remember that each individual has his/her own time schedule in this process. Also many of these feelings are overlapping and contradictory. We may feel one at a time, notice a succession of several, or experience many feelings concurrently. Some individuals may not experience all of these manifestations, and this too is normal. If we experience one, several, or all of these manifestations of grief, it may or may not be a measure of our degree of suffering. We are each unique in this regard and individuality must be revered with no judgements on how anyone <u>should</u> feel.

The grieving process is interwoven within the art of healing. Grieving is healing as suffering is grace. Awareness is the key. Educating our culture to the many realities of psychological pain and suffering, the splintering of the soul, is how we will arrive at a more compassionate and loving society which recognizes that the human experience encompasses the BOTH/AND reality of the soul's journey. The many paths toward healing are inclusive of *being in the suffering* and *going through the grieving*.

During my process of healing, I often felt abandoned by the experts when they told me to grieve, but no one told me how this was done. My intent, while recognizing this is an individual journey, is to shed some light on this area of neglect. I have decided that by disclosing my process within each of the manifestations of grief, this will help others. My experience with group dynamics leads me to believe that emotions have a more universal feeling than we've admitted in the past. This awareness comes from sitting in twelve-step meetings every week for over five years and listening. I listened with my mind and heart while everyone in the room (including myself) wrestled with the demons of our souls. I learned through this process that I was not alone, that others felt as I did. When they shared their personal stories, I was able to relate and identify my feelings, giving them names for the first time. This was the beginning of my climb out of my abyss of darkness. And, as we recover, we share our hope, strength, and courage which is a form of selfless service. This is why twelve-step programs work. Sharing our universal...ness, instead of insisting on our different...ness, unites us and helps us to heal.

The hospice philosophy works in a similar fashion. Though it is not a prerequisite to have lost a loved one to become a bereavement volunteer, more often than not that is the case. Because we have lost someone, we understand and have compassion for those whom we assist. By revealing our losses to our clients, it lets them know that we, too, have suffered pain and that they are not alone.

A dichotomy arises for me as I hear the experts indicate that we should never say to the bereaved, "I know how you feel." And personally, I have had clients and students share that, when people say this to them, it makes them angry. It may not be politically correct, but I must demystify this notion. I believe the bereaved feel this way because they read it in all the books. Or, it may be due to the fact that in the self-indulgent vulnerability of grief, we need to feel different from others so we can realize our pain. Whichever it is, I think it causes many people to isolate and suffer in silence. It makes us feel abnormal or pathological. It separates us from others when, in the crisis of our pain, what we really need is to feel closer to others.

When we realize that others *do* know how we feel, a special bonding emerges that strengthens our healing process. As I assist bereaved families, you can be assured that I know how they feel. I lost my father to alcoholism, my mother to spousal abuse, a sister to anorexia, another sister to a brain aneurysm, a niece to child abuse, a husband to divorce after a thirty-year relationship, and a certain degree of physical mobility due to the near-death experience of my auto accident. So, I do know how they feel. Clients report to me, as I share my stories of loss, that my disclosure is what gives them permission to face their own truths and feelings. They recognize that I do know how they feel due to my experiences of loss and grief. I know that change is often scary and many of us simply refuse and/or are uncomfortable in accepting change. Please reconsider the idea that "others don't know how we feel" and give ourselves permission to say, "I do know how you feel."

However, it is inappropriate and irresponsible to use this new freedom of disclosure—"I know how you feel"—if one truly doesn't know how the other person feels. If we have not had a similar loss (i.e., death of a loved one, rape, homelessness, or dealing with daily physical or mental illness, job loss, etc.), then we <u>do not</u> know how the victim or survivor feels. And, we should not presume that we do because this would be a violation of honoring their pain and suffering. So it is only valid if we have had the same experience, if we have personally been there. Of course, everyone has their own attitudes, beliefs, and unique personality; therefore, no two experiences are exactly the same. Still, my experience tells me they are more alike than different. I believe in being authentic. Sharing authentic experiences is a profound ingredient of the healing process. As one becomes an authentic exemplar, every intention and action transcends the self and becomes a matter of selfless service—a service of love and compassion for all of humanity and the world we live in. The remainder of this chapter expresses my understanding of the manifestations of grief.

Denial

Denial is often judged as having a negative connotation. I believe that it serves us individually and collectively in a positive way. When our loss or devastating situation/condition is initially experienced, we need the buffer of our ego's denial until the human mind can assimilate what is happening to the entire organism. Denial is normal and spirals in and out of the experience as long as we have to deal with the situation. We see this as a first reaction by those faced with terminal illness; and I experienced denial with regard to the family disease of alcoholism.

The psyche can only handle the reality of pain and suffering in bits and pieces—"little moments at a time," as Ram Dass put it. Denial is temporary and the psyche's way of coping with traumatic events. I see it as only being dangerous when we stay too long in our denial, blocking our conscious awareness of our reality. We also need moments of clarity and vulnerable awareness if we are to learn and grow from the experience. There is a time for denial and a time for dropping our mask to see the light. We must be patient with ourselves and one another in this regard.

Emotional Outburst

Emotional outbursts are common, especially in the early months of our grief. This form of release may be experienced as anger/rage or as outbursts of sobbing and tears. Acknowledging anger, if we feel any, is necessary and must be managed appropriately. Talking it out with a trusted friend, counselor or support person is beneficial so that we do not repress our anger or project it onto others in acts of inappropriate behavior, as is so often the case. Those closest to us usually bear the brunt of such behavior, resulting in more pain and suffering.

Anger does not sit comfortably in my heart and soul. Because of this, I repressed it for years causing all kinds of health problems.

130 It is imperative that we work through anger. Anger is a negative energy that breeds more anger and has many physical, social, psychological, and spiritual repercussions as noted by Dr. Daniel Goleman in his enlightening book, *Emotional Intelligence.*[5] Anger blocks the free-flowing positive energies of love and compassion.

Crying and tears are healthy and healing ways of cleansing the soul. Crying changes the physiology of the human organism and releases any built up tension in the body. Unfortunately, many of us (especially men) have been socialized to believe that crying displays a weakness in character and/or a lack of strength and courage. It takes more courage to embrace and express your feelings, than to restrain them. Crying will not bring the loved ones or lost object back into earthly reality, but it helps to bring the survivor back—back in touch with his/her heart and soul.

I have several hospice clients who have had awful experiences after they have returned to work. Their employers and fellow coworkers didn't understand their sudden and unexpected emotional outbursts of tears. Education is needed so we can be more sensitive and compassionate to loss, giving people the time they need to grieve and heal. Our social standard seems to dictate that we bury our loved one and return to work within days, wearing a smiling face. This is absurd and cruel. We must also have the heart to recognize that these manifestations of grief can occur with all losses, not just death.

Sleep and Eating Disturbances

The grief process may entail sleeplessness, which is normal at first, as our sense of loss and strong emotions invade our mind during both waking and sleeping hours. Mental confusion and lack of ability to focus or concentrate are common manifestations of grief. Naturally, we become preoccupied with our loss.

Eating patterns often get disrupted as well causing weight loss or gain. Though these manifestations are normal during the first days and even weeks, we must remain aware of these issues. If disturbed sleeping and eating habits continue for very long, they compound our grief as our health and well-being suffer. If we do not get enough rest, sleep, and nourishment, we may be headed for serious physical, mental, and psychological problems.

The dangers of a change in eating habits are subtle and gradual. During times of extreme grief or pain and suffering due to ego-developmental stages and other losses, such as those associated with family dysfunction due to drug and alcohol addiction and/or sexual abuse, we may find ourselves in the throes of more serious eating disorders, including anorexia or bulimia. At a time in our life when everything seems crazy and out of our control, we may unconsciously find some sense of control in our eating habits. Overeating may temporarily appear to bring us comfort. Please do not be ashamed to consult your family physician during your grieving/healing process to discuss your reactions to your loss. This is an act of love for one's self.

Pain and Anguish

Deep pain, hurting down in the pit of our solar plexus or sometimes throughout our whole body, is a common reaction to a sudden shock and loss. We all know the familiar expressions "heartache" or "broken heart." Our soul cries out in turmoil as our heart feels like it has had its life force taken from it. This pain of the heart and soul feels physical, but it is actually caused by a deprivation of spirit. We may feel distraught or in deep anguish. We are lost in our despair. These are debilitating feelings of unwholeness which signal that the human organism is not in its holistic balance.

Other physical pain may spiral in and out for a time. I know people who suffer with mild stomachaches or headaches during grief. We must remember, we are under a lot of stress. Breathing and relaxation techniques, practiced adjunctively with biofeedback and somatic movements, can assist us with these mild to severe symptoms. These healing techniques will be discussed in the next chapter.

Grief may alter our physiology as the central nervous system prepares itself to handle stress—the fight or flight response. If we remain in a state of hyperalertness for long periods of time, we can develop high blood pressure, migraine headaches, heart and respiratory problems, gastrointestinal complications, and more. Remember my friend Margaret, who developed insulin dependant diabetes directly after the death of her son? Please listen to your body and give yourself permission to see your family physician, even if you are not displaying physical symptoms or discomfort. It is wise to have a checkup just as a security measure.

Restlessness and Impatience

Restlessness is common during both the sleeping and waking states. When our whole world has been turned upside down, it is normal to feel restless and impatient with the grieving/healing process. We must trust ourselves and the process, as sometimes this is all we have to get us through our traumatic life events. Give yourself permission to be out of sorts. Then give yourself permission for an even longer healing process and trust that it will get better.

Ambiguity and Apathy

If we feel ambiguous or ambivalent about life during grief, it is probably due to the fact that nothing makes sense to us anymore. We may lose a further sense of trust, reason, or purpose and become vague about our relationships, unsure about life's meaning. We don't understand why these things happen, and it makes us feel impotent. We may become apathetic, indifferent, unconcerned. These feelings may pertain to certain areas of our life or to life in general. Some of us feel that nothing matters anymore.

If you find yourself experiencing these feelings, please talk to someone, and work through it. Education is available to help us understand our feelings, or in this case, lack of feelings.

Low Self-Esteem

Anytime we go through loss, change, and grief it can affect our sense of self-esteem or self-worth. We feel splintered, broken, unwhole. Regaining one's sense of self and sense of purpose is usually a slow process. Be patient. Personally, I was unaware that my sense of self was only identified with my social self. Due to my losses in the area of ego-development during adolescence, I only knew how to gauge my self-worth through the roles of wife and mother. I put all my energies into trying to measure up to what I thought society dictated as the perfect model of these roles.

Of course, what happens when we do this is that we set ourselves up for failure. No one is perfect; we are human. These idealized roles are fabrications of a false persona. Our outer personality is therefore different from our true self which lies within our heart and soul. I thought if I were nice enough, worked hard enough, and loved others enough that I would be happy and they would love me back. But I was miserable and didn't know why. I have since come to know that, though all of these personality traits are good ones, my splinteredness was due to the fact that I was trying to find wholeness (my Holistic Self) through the love, approval, and acceptance of others. It took me five years to become comfortable with my inner self which reconnected me to God and provided me with love of self. This healing process was about searching deep within my heart and soul to feel my spirit. As I did this I learned to accept my wonderful qualities and my not-so-wonderful qualities. It is about taking responsibility for one's own happiness.

134

Guilt and Shame

As with all the manifestations of grief, guilt appears in waves or spirals in and out of the healing process, affecting us to varying degrees and at various levels. Naturally, we cannot excuse any egregious acts against each other in our discussion of guilt and shame. Appropriate or healthy shame for the mistakes we make in life is a matter of taking responsibility for our actions and behaviors. As we work through our grief of life's challenges, we learn to take responsibility for both our healthy and unhealthy choices. This is not about blame or fault. Blame, fault, and guilt are negative energies that bring about more pain and suffering.

Because we are beings of both worlds, the material and the spiritual, we are going to make mistakes. This is necessary for growth. We must own our mistakes or shortcomings without harboring any unnecessary sense of guilt. This awareness enables us to make amends and change our behaviors to show that we have learned from our errors. It takes more strength and courage to face the conflicting aspects of the soul than to allow our ego to mask our perceptions. Balancing the energies of your shadow and persona will bring you a sense of wholeness and peace.

In grief work, what we most often witness is the guilt of bereaved individuals who blame themselves for not having done enough to prevent the terminal illness or death of a loved one. I see this as an inflated sense of ego that suggests we have control over such things. If we really feel we could have prevented these losses we must have an exaggerated sense of self-importance and power. Remember it is not what happens to us but what we *do* with what happens to us. If we handle loss and separation by harboring guilt, we take on inappropriate self-destructiveness. We are punishing ourselves unnecessarily. Terminal illness, death, natural disaster, job loss, etc., are not our fault. We do not need to feel ashamed if there is mental or physical illness in our self or in our families. We do need to take responsibility for how we deal with all these challenges of being human. An example of this is Christopher Reeve's expressed awareness of his suffering and healing process: "We don't look at our limitations, we look at our opportunities."[6]

Another thing that I have discovered is why I carried unnecessary guilt and shame. When situations were out of my control, it became easier to own part of the problem than to be part of the solution. Unconsciously, I was taking responsibility and blame for the sadness and emotional discomfort in my family, hoping it relieved the other person's (be it spouse or child) pain and suffering. This was not true. It only complicated the situation. We cannot and should not deprive others of their suffering because, when we do, we rob them of their healing and personal growth process. As a parent this is hard to do as we want to spare or ease our children's pain. I have learned that we must allow them to experience their own feelings of hurt and disappointment. This shows respect and love for one another.

When we suffer with self-inflicted guilt over not having treated people decently before we lost them, we are missing the opportunity to enjoy their presence in our lives. Grief is about showing reverence for the other person's journey, not a time for self-absorption. Hopefully, through our healing process, we learn how to treat people with respect and kindness while they are alive, instead of after they are gone.

Sort out what is and what is not your responsibility. Be gentle with yourself. Let go of the rest. Do the best you can and continue to learn and grow. If you really feel you have made a mistake, make amends in new ways. It's about discovering the positive within the negative. It is about choosing to look at life as the glass being half full, not half empty. It is about finding new meaning and purpose in all the challenges of life. Do not limit yourself—use the sorrows of your journey as opportunities for awareness and as roads towards wholeness—healing the Holistic Self so as to hold hands with unity consciousness.

Loneliness and Abandonment

Feelings of abandonment are real and cause all kinds of fears to surface. When we are abandoned, we lose a sense of attachment and belonging to something larger than self. I felt more lonely the last five years of my marriage than I have since I've been single. My heart ached as I felt the presence of my husband's mistress between us—the mistress of alcohol. Loneliness may occur in the presence of others because there is an emotional void. Neither of us could give ourselves permission to feel love; we had closed our hearts to self and each other. Since then I have filled my void with the presence of Spirit, and I no longer feel lonely. The Divine Spirit or God does not abandon us; we abandon the Spirit. We are only abandoned by ourselves and those things (or people) of the material world. Once we become whole, engaged in living in the presence of our Holistic

136

Self, we will not experience loneliness. We will have open hearts and be able to feel love.

Depression and Isolation

It seems to be a human tendency to withdraw or isolate ourselves after we have experienced a loss. This is a mistake. When love or our sense of connectedness has been taken from us, what we need is the companionship and closeness of others. Respecting that we also need some private time for reflection and sacred remembrances, we must not isolate ourselves from the rest of the world. When we find ourselves withdrawing from rather than participating in life, we must pick up the phone and connect with the life force of humanity. A support person or group is comforting as we work through our depression, for the simple reason that we do not always have the energy to do it by ourselves. Others cannot minister to our needs if we do not allow them in.

I agree with Deepak Chopra, David R. Dietrich, and Peter C. Shabad who feel that depression is a lack of love or a loss of meaning in one's life. Freud said that there are two things of importance in life—love and work. Both our love relationships and our life work are what give our life meaning—our earthly essence.

Depression has many causes, degrees of intensity, and diagnostic components. It may result from chemical imbalances in the brain, which I believe can be created as the human organism attempts to cope with stress. We can be suffering from depression and not even realize it. The depression or despondency that accompanies grief is usually mild and a natural response to our loss. Depression is often referred to as "low spirits," an apt description. If we isolate ourselves with a sense of helplessness or hopelessness for long periods of time, we may become chronically depressed, which requires psychological and/or medical attention.

The depression of grief is really a healing tool. Like all the manifestations of loss and grief, it signals that our psyche (soul) is out of balance. I embraced my depression after my divorce, allowing it to comfort my melancholy. This was a sacred gift, as it gave me the opportunity to reflect on my feelings. It was through this process that I got in touch with my soul. As I allowed myself to feel my pain, I began to identify my emotions. Naming them as sadness, anger, loneliness, etc., resulted in a profound awareness of what I might do to work through them. Paradoxically, if depression is a low of spirits, it is through embracing it that we return to a high point or fullness of spirit. Before we know it, our depression leaves us.

Helplessness and Hopelessness

I can only restate the wisdom of one of my students who said, "Helplessness is when we have given up on others and hopelessness is when we have given up on ourselves." A sense of helplessness occurs when one does not know how, who, or what to reach out for in our attempt to lift the despair of darkness. We may feel others don't care enough about us to help, or that we do not want to bother others with our pain. Helplessness and hopelessness often go hand in hand with depression.[7] When we are feeling as though we cannot go on due to the change or trauma in our life, low self-esteem may rear its ugly head. Hopelessness indicates a sense that there is no reason to go on, no reason to live. Reach out and ask for help and you will receive it. This is your responsibility. In this way we accept our soul's need for a reconnection with the spirit of others. Honoring the soul puts us in touch with the creativity of the Spirit, which will help us out of our sorrow.

Sadness and Missing...ness

It is natural and normal to be deeply saddened over our losses, be they object loss or body loss. It is important not to deny ourselves this reality of sadness, because our sadness is real. We also recognize that gladness or happiness is the opposite of the soul's sadness and that we may experience both. If we see someone else who is less fortunate with painful conditions of life, it is normal to feel grateful that we are not suffering as they are. It is also human to be relieved that people transcend their pain and suffering, moving on to the other world. So do not chastise yourself when rays of happiness, gladness, or gratitude spiral in and out of your grief/healing process. It is normal to experience these feelings.

I felt this way when my mother died. I was truly saddened by her death but at the same time glad that she no longer had to suffer her hell of domestic violence here on earth. I miss my mother more today than I did twenty years ago. It is normal and natural that, as we age, we become more aware of our immortality, reminding us of our losses. We miss what could have been and yearn for our loved one's presence in our mortal life. I'm saddened that my mother isn't here to share my relationship with my daughters. I am even sadder that she did not get the opportunity to share her love and wisdom with all her grand-children. Using the acronym, MISS, I impart to my students that missing those whom we have lost is a celebration of their importance to us. Here is a fun mnemonic:

Memories
I lluminate
S acred
S tories

When we miss someone or something we are really keeping them alive in our hearts. During the healing process, the cold-ness of missing someone becomes the warmth of ministering to our soul.

On holidays, anniversary dates, and birthdays (all occasions of celebration) we feel more vulnerable. Our moments of joy re-mind us of our loss and we become very sad, oftentimes feeling guilty for our rejoicing in the happy occasion. This, too, is normal. It is natural to miss our loved ones or our old ways of attachment to self in previous relationships. Allow yourself time for reflection, remembrances, and sadness for your loss and grief. We will always miss our loved ones, just to a different degree. Our pain will be manageable. But do not feel guilty because you are still alive and enjoying the festivities of these special dates. Create new rituals and new ways of celebrating these sacred events; make them a new beginning. Find the creative spirit within that will assist you in healing your sadness and missingness.

Through this dichotomy presented to us by the emotional polarity of the soul, we begin to understand healing as both psychological death and rebirth—a moving forward in the dance of life. By being happy and grateful for our blessings in life, we show appreciation and reverence for GRACE. The BOTH/AND concept of the soul demands that the human experience is about a beingness of both happiness and sadness.

Fear and Resistance

I believe that fear is at the root of unhappiness and emotional pain and suffering. Fear is the powerful axe that splinters the soul. Throughout my book I have suggested that it is when we get stuck in our pain and suffering that it leaves the realm of normal grief and becomes pathological. This reality of being stuck is our resistance to change. Just as loss, separation, anxiety, and grief are about change, healing is also about change. Human resistance to change is an expression of fear and, unfortunately, an aspect of human beingness. The antithesis of fear is freedom.

The grieving process has many variables. In this chapter I have discussed the physiological, mental, psychosocial, and spiritual

140

manifestations of grief that spiral in and out of the human experience. Healing from the reference point of the soul, instead of the socialized ego, gives us the gift of spirit. With this grace, we have the courage to make choices that realign all the properties and roles which make up the Holistic Self. We really cannot love others until we truly love ourselves—our spiritual-self not our ego-self. When we love the spirit of self, we connect to ALL that is. We integrate our material, social, and spiritual selves that keep our energies in balance and enjoy a renewed sense of wholeness.

Due to my metamorphosis I am now able to take responsibility for changing the parts of my ego-self that brought me discomfort. We each have the power and creativity to do this. I indicated in earlier chapters that healing was a sacred journey of self-discovery. Through the hills and valleys of this exploration we become aware of the mystery in both the death and rebirth of life. Yes, I learned to celebrate life with all its sense of unfairness, pain, and suffering. I now understand that the human experience is about both. I walk forward with a renewed sense of purpose and gratitude for all that I am and all that I have. I did this by removing the layers of psychological pain and suffering (artichoke metaphor) of my soul around all my losses and grief. Overcoming my fear of death has liberated me; now, I can soar with the eagles.

> *Being a hero is about discovering our human divinity—that powerful, creative source that we each have within us— and living by it.*
> —Lorna Catford & Michael Ray

> *When you confront your mortality, you begin to notice that there is a lifetime to create.*
> —Eleanor Criswell

10

From Darkness to Light (Choosing a Path)

> Say not, "I have found the path of the soul." Say rather, "I have met the soul walking upon my path." For the soul walks upon all paths...The soul unfolds itself, like a lotus of countless petals.
>
> —Kahlil Gibran

> Intention is the active partner of attention; it is the way we convert automatic processes into conscious ones.
>
> —Deepak Chopra

The process of reorganization is difficult for many of us. This is where I believe further education and assistance is needed. When we become aware that there are many paths through our grief, it begins our transformation out of psychological pain and suffering to a lighter place of renewed energy. Recognizing the polarities of the soul as a union of opposite energies, we understand that grief, stress, and anxiety are aspects of the *darker* side of the soul, while at the same time, love, compassion, peace, hope, forgiveness, and acceptance are equally powerful aspects of the *lighter* side of the soul. This spiritual or light side of the soul is our saving grace, which offers the gifts of healing and balance to the human psyche.

It is through human pain and suffering that we get the opportunity to change and grow, thus learning to celebrate life. Thomas Moore says, "In our attempt, as psychologists, to alleviate suffering we must observe what is being revealed in the suffering."[1] Whether we're the soul doctor who assists others with their grievances or the individual observing his/her own suffering, what we are doing in essence is cultivating the desires of the soul. Observation by the conscious mind will help us to open our hearts to our creative or divine self which will assist us in returning to a place of homeostasis.

My personal experiences, integrated with what I have learned from Kubler-Ross about the dying process and the angelic caring demonstrated by the hospice phenomena, suggest that to transcend our grief we must come to a place of acceptance. This is easier said than done, but each of us, with our individual uniqueness, can slowly and reverently learn how to do this. Personally, I have used and continue to use all these coping mechanisms, as the human experience is an infinite reality of both suffering and celebrating life. As grief spirals in and out of our lives, healing is an ongoing process of oscillating waves of energy, giving us a sense of release from our pain and suffering.

143

Talk Therapy

We must talk about our feelings, be it with a private counselor or a dear friend. Talking out our troubles releases the angst from our mind, body, and soul. If we keep negative emotions and thoughts repressed in our unconscious minds and the cells of our bodies, we create additional stress or pain and suffering. Negative energy is released as we verbalize our deepest fears, feelings, and thoughts. It is imperative that we reach out to others and share our stories of sadness. Bonding with others creates a transfer of energy; our family and friends give us the energy of strength, hope, and courage to move forward. This exchange is reciprocal and both parties receive love. Of course, we must select someone who is trustworthy as this is about the intimacy of our hearts. Support groups relating to your specific loss are good choices as these special individuals understand your pain. An example of this would be support groups created especially for cancer survivors, those who live with HIV/AIDS, twelve-step recovery programs, or bereavement counseling from your local hospice when your loss is the death of a loved one.

Listening

Being a good listener teaches us to be empathetic and compassionate. Humanistic psychologist Carl Rogers emphasizes the benefits of "positive regard" for others which is a demonstration of respect in honoring the other person's experience, listening with both our minds and our hearts. Active listening requires SOUL. Each party receives grace from this exchange of love and respect. Empathetic listening reveals what is being expressed in the pain and suffering. One of the greatest gifts we can give anyone who is in despair is to be a good listener. If we also practice the art of *silence*, we will discover clarity of mind and other blessings.

Journaling or Writing

Journaling is a tool with which many people are not comfortable. As a teacher and bereavement group leader, I stress the healing that comes with writing. Writing is a creative process that puts us in touch with the emotions of the soul. Like talk therapy, it is a means of releasing negative energies. Journaling is a way of recording our feelings and thoughts so that we may return to them for purpose of contemplation and reflection. Simply put, writing helps us sort things out.

I found that through the writing process, the intensity of my grief and feelings began to dissipate. They became more

Listening

144

Writing

manageable. Writing is an excellent way to deal with anger. As we put our anger onto paper, it draws it away from our mind, body, and soul. My father died before I dealt with all my anger and distorted thinking from childhood. Though he had passed to the other world, I wrote him letters to assist me in minimizing my pain. I have also written letters to my mother to say the loving things I needed to say to her and never got the chance. Your notes or letters can be written to others, deceased or living, or to yourself. Writing or journaling is an exercise of transforming energy. Also, because paper can easily be burned, we can keep our thoughts private. Some revelations are too threatening or intimate to share with others; writing them down and burning them up hurts no one but will help us cleanse our hearts.

Your Personal Biography

145

The Hospice Foundation of America suggests to the terminally ill that they write or have someone help them write a personal story. This process can help relieve pain and suffering and can also serve as a recorded genealogy for family and friends to memorialize our human journey. Writing our personal history assists us in putting our life's journey into a new light or healthier perspective. This autobiographical task is about remembering both the sadness and the joyousness of life. Much is revealed as the truth unfolds, and these memoirs help those who are about to make their transition to the other world bring closure to the time-bound awareness of this physical world. By celebrating our journey—reviewing the failures and successes of our experiences and coming to a place of acceptance—we acknowledge that we did the best we could and champion the Holistic Self.

This biography does not have to be lengthy. Do not let the process intimidate or scare you. You may choose to do it in bits and pieces. You may choose the oral tradition instead of the written one. The process, not the method, is what's important.

The format may be a short poem or story, a novel or a volume of facts; one page, ten pages, or a hundred. Storytelling, whether it be verbal or written, is an excellent way of caring for the soul.[2]

Art Work

Art therapy is used frequently today to help understand the mysteries of the soul. Remember a wide variety of creative media can help in healing our splinteredness. Along with music and meditative relaxation techniques, I use drawing to assist my clients and students in expressing their emotions. We use crayons and colorful markers to let our feelings flow. Color, shape, and symbols give language and meaning to one's soul.[3] We do not have to be a Rembrandt or Michelangelo. It is about accessing the creative artist within the Divine Self.[4] I have also found it helpful to make mandalas (circular designs) or collages using words, symbols, pictures, and/or any artifacts which have meaning for the one creating them.

Music and Poetry

Music and poetry are art forms which soothe the heart as we tend to our soul. Healing comes from creating music by playing an instrument, dancing or singing, or by listening and watching all forms of music and music making. During the grieving/ healing process of my divorce, country line dancing became very therapeutic for me. Learning the steps helped to realign the rhythmic energies of my body while giving me the chance to be with people in a joyous environment. Going to the dances kept me from isolating myself and reminded me to participate in living. Dancing is a wonderful form of physical exercise and helps to rid us of depression and the blues of loss and grief.

Reading poetry nurtures the heart. I write poetry as a means of expressing both the sadness of my soul and the peace and beauty

146

Art Work

Music and Poetry

of my heart. This is a healing process that I invite each of you to try. Like the soul, poetry has dualistic qualities: comforting depression on one hand, and rejoicing euphoria on the other.

Dreams

During our grief, we often experience more active dream recall. Dreams are messengers of healing. When writing them down and sharing them with friends and family, we discover insight into the message, which we might otherwise miss. Healing is an process of self-discovery, and as Carl Jung and others have noted, dreams unlock the mystery of the unconscious mind. Bereaved clients have entrusted me with their dreams, and in some cases, *visions* of their loved ones. Many people find great comfort in this world of magic and mystery. Keeping a dream journal and analyzing our dreams can reveal much about the self, help in the healing process, and be lots of fun.

Reading and Movies

A good novel is not only relaxing but helps us to redirect our attention to something outside our self. Reading can also be a source of education and awareness, especially in the area of death and bereavement. My clients report that they receive tremendous comfort in reading how others have adjusted to loss and regained a sense of meaning and purpose.

Going to movies gets us off the couch and out of the house. Sad movies give us permission to have a good cry, which we might not otherwise do. Funny movies lift our spirits and help us to realize that life is about joy and having a good time. Laughter, like tears, is cleansing, and both are sacred gifts of the soul. It is okay to laugh; we are not dishonoring our loss or loved one if we have moments of joy and laughter. Giving ourselves permission to laugh, sing, and dance renews our Spirit even in the darkest of hours.

Nature

Mother Nature offers us opportunities for healing in many ways. Her beautiful gifts of a sunrise or sunset, the forest, mountains, desert, and breathtaking oceans give us peace and serenity—indeed a spiritual rebirth. Listening to the rain can comfort our melancholy. Watching the clouds by day and the stars by night help us to put things in a more profound perspective. We can reconnect to the cosmic and universal sense of All, knowing we are alive and part of the sacred mystery.

We can experience nature as we tend to our physical wellbeing by taking walks. Exercise is one of our better tools for coping with stress and depression. I cannot emphasize strongly enough the benefits of moderate and continuous exercise as it heals the mind, body, and soul. You will be surprised as to the healing qualities of these natural remedies. A simple twenty- to thirty-minute walk a day (if you can only do it for five minutes, then do it for five minutes) helps to clear the mind, unravel the stressed nerves, and balance our physical energies.

148

Another tip I find helpful during times of stress is to drink water. Water helps to purify the body, essential in maintaining good health. If we neglect our physical health, our mind and spirit suffer to a greater degree.

Many clients have shared that gardening is an excellent healing tool. Planting in the richness of Mother Earth's soil and harvesting the fruits of one's labor remind us of the ongoing reality of the life cycle. These ordinary, daily activities are ways of ministering to the soul during our grieving/healing process.

Hobbies

We all need hobbies to balance out the responsibilities of life. Golf, fishing, bowling, and all kinds of sports are part of tending to the needs of the soul. Many of us find comfort and self-expression in cooking or baking, sewing or crocheting. Quilt making is a wonderful therapy and is becoming popular again. The families of AIDS patients pay tribute to their loved ones in the creative design of memorial quilts. Once again, reading, music, poetry, theatre, and the arts can offer entertainment and diversion. All of these hobbies are strategies for coping with life's disappointments. Be imaginative and find your bliss in whatever makes you happy and brings you home to your inner self. Spirit lies deep within each of us and is awaiting our call to help us heal and return to balance.

Prayer and Meditation

I have found much comfort through both prayer and meditation. Sant Rajinder Singh, president of the World Fellowship of Religion and the spiritual head of Science of Spirituality, said, "Prayer is when we are talking to God...Meditation is when we listen to God."[5] I find this statement to be profoundly true. I talk to God, my ancestors in the spirit-world, and my guardian angels daily as I sort out my life, asking for guidance, strength, wisdom, patience, and the courage to deal with my challenges, especially that of living in constant pain from my spinal cord injury. This contemplative practice reminds me there is a higher wisdom than that which I have alone. Meditation is an opening up to unity consciousness of all energy. I also pray with reverence and gratitude, mindful of and with heartfelt appreciation for all that I am.

Once I learned to meditate, a whole new awareness of healing opened up to me. The silence and reverence of quieting mind, body, and soul serve to unify all aspects of my Holistic Self. In the grace of silence I am rewarded with listening to God, and this is such a sacred experience that it is difficult to describe. I become connected to unity consciousness, which mysteriously and magically whispers what part of the Holistic Self is out of balance and needs my loving attention. If we listen with our heart, we realize we are in a synthesis of mind, body, soul, and spirit; we realize that our answers lie within the self. Meditation reconnects us to our soul, making us aware that we are of the Spirit. There are many different but equally effective approaches to prayer and meditation; only personal choice determines which is right for each of us.

Yoga, in its various forms, is an excellent medium for bringing us into balance so that we can open up to the heart of Spirit. Buddha expressed that meditation is not enlightenment but a *way* to enlightenment. Meditation brings forth and/or allows for awareness and mental clarity. We can use these esoteric practices in healing the very real pain and suffering of humanity.

Another practice of devotion resides in the many religious and nonreligious rituals and observances practiced by all humankind. After the death of a loved one, bereaved clients report that visits to the cemetery or erecting an altar in their homes in memory of their loved one bring them comfort and peace. I have such an altar and wasn't aware of it until I heard it expressed in these terms by my clients. On a small table sitting near my piano are pictures of my mother and two sisters (Mary, who died of anorexia, and Pat, who died of an aneurysm), a candle, and flowers. As I play sweet music, memories and love sing in my heart.

In this decade, the prelude to a new millennium, we hear of many moving stories where people encounter angelic intervention. I believe that angels are our most significant connections to the other world, the spiritual realm, and are present in our lives helping us as we struggle with the illusion of being in our physical bodies. Saint Thomas Aquinas said, "We are like children, who stand in need of masters to enlighten us and direct us; and God has provided for this, by appointing his angels to be our teachers and guides."[6] I feel, too, that there are special people walking amongst us in human form who are truly angels. There have been several people in my life who qualify for this sacred honor.

Human Interaction

Human interaction is a necessary component of healing our splintered soul. The greatest gift we can give anyone in his or her time of psychological suffering is our presence, love, and respect. Being present or witness to our pain or that of others is a sacred experience. Many times we don't know what to say or do to assist others. Just being by their side is what is most important. "I'm sorry" and "How can I help you?" are the words they need to hear. Our silence and listening gives the grieving individual the opportunity to contemplate his or her pain and suffering. Crying and laughing together releases tension, and with their permission, a hug is usually both needed and appreciated.

To some extent, families share their grief, but sometimes this is difficult. Often, family members need an outsider to confide in, which is normal and understandable. Sometimes we are too close to the situation and need to work through our grief with others. As I have previously mentioned, we need a good support system—be it friends, a counselor, or support groups. When we attempt to go through our grief alone, we often make it worse. Reach out to others and let their love assist you in your healing. Human interaction reminds us that we are alive. If we share our grievances and anxieties, we will not become isolated, hopeless, and depressed. Socializing brings a sense of warmth and joy into our lives and provides much-needed diversion, giving us respite from our sorrows. It is crucial that we connect with others.

As the support person or friend, we have much to offer. Phone calls, cards and notes, meal invitations, respite care, baby-sitting, and all the caring and thoughtful things that we would like, we can give to others.[7] Be a true friend and stay for the long haul. Sharing experiences can be a gift, creating a bond of love.

Selfless service is soul work. When we give of ourselves, without any expectations of reciprocity, then we are giving from the heart of Spirit. This is an act of grace and rewards all. If we are the support person, we put ourselves in the service of others. If we are the one grieving, give ourselves to others as this helps us to heal. This is about going outside the ego-self and connecting with the Divine Self. This is about the omnipotent power and miracle of love.

Hope

I believe that all our life experiences affect and change us; therefore, we are never the same again. We have a choice to look at the positive within the negative. As we grow from our experiences, we see things in a new light, which makes it easier to move forward and appreciate the mystery. Know that you are not alone and suffering is universal. After my daughter's victimization, she was able to put her grief and fears in a different perspective as she witnessed the plight of those whose pain and suffering were greater than hers, helping her to heal. We must not abandon hope.

Patience and Tolerance

Patience with the process is an act of trust. Be patient with your developing self and be patient with your fellow human beings. This is a hard concept for most of us to practice in daily living. Constantly, I work on having patience with myself, and having patience with others as we all grow to a place of peace and enlightenment. Healing is a lifelong process of growth, individually and collectively. When we practice patience and acceptance, we become tolerant. Tolerance begets tolerance, which has a profound, overwhelming ripple effect touching all aspects of humanity.

Forgiveness

My personal experience with forgiveness—another hard-to-define concept—really comes back to self. I have learned that though I kept trying to forgive my father, it was not until I could

152

forgive myself that I could truly forgive him and others. Paradoxically, forgiveness of others requires forgiveness of self. After twenty-some years of working on forgiveness, I realized that I did not have to forgive my father for his unspeakable crime. Really it is not my place—a larger power or force must balance this seemingly unjust behavior. What I did minister to was forgiveness around the issue of neglect and emotional abuse in the father-daughter relationship. This is an ongoing practice of forgiveness as these issues seem to resurface periodically.

Healing is about letting go of things we cannot control and taking responsibility for and acting on the things we can change. We can change ourselves. We cannot change others. Forgive others who have caused you pain as this is an act of love—an act of love for both the self and others. Forgiveness is really a decision to move on. Forgiveness is about freedom, about freeing yourself from the emotional pain of the past. It is about letting go of the past and living in the present. It is an act of healing the pain and suffering of the splintered soul. As I learned to forgive myself for the mistakes I had made being wife and mother, I was able to forgive others for their mistakes, including my father. Healing is about honoring that we are from both worlds.

Acceptance

Elisabeth Kubler-Ross suggests that acceptance is the last stage of the dying process. Witnessing this level of consciousness, as the terminally ill prepare for their transformation to the other world, gives those of us living in the material world a profound gift. I apply this wisdom to grieving and healing our ordinary losses. I believe that it is when we remain stuck in our grief that it can become pathological. We have a choice to remain victims or to become survivors. We have a choice to accept or deny our conditions of the material world. In choosing how we cope with our angst and sadness, we determine how we will enjoy and celebrate life.

When we arrive at a place of acceptance, then we can make changes that will help us to let go of what we cannot affect and move forward to that which we can. This is about freedom, respect, and living with meaning or purpose or dying with dignity and honor. Acceptance is the last stage of the dying process; paradoxically, it is the first stage of the living process—being able to really live life.

Letting go, surrender, and acceptance are concepts many of us resist. They make us feel defeated or victimized. But this is not the meaning of acceptance as defined by Kubler-Ross. As explained in Judith Viorst's book, *Necessary Losses*, the meaning of acceptance, according to Kubler-Ross, "should not be mistaken for a happy phase." Instead, "It is almost void of feelings…a time when the struggle is done."[8] This is exactly how I regard acceptance. In my own case, I was too exhausted, splintered, drained of energy, afraid, and I did not have any more answers or ego-coping mechanisms to sustain the struggle. Alcohol, which I denied for years, could no longer mask the demons of my soul. I was now ready to surrender to God, let go of the past, and *accept* whatever path He showed me. This was necessary if I was to ever live in peace. In a true sense, it was a big relief, knowing I no longer carried the burden by myself.

When I quit drinking, I began my journey of ministering to the heart of my fragile psyche. After two years of sobriety and conscious efforts of trying to find a sense of self, I came to a place of acceptance that my marriage was over. Part of me felt that if I couldn't make this relationship work, nothing in my life would work. I was confused as I surrendered to "not having all the answers" to my destiny. Letting go of the past, letting go of future expectations, and living in the present moment gave me back my sanity. I began to realize that the human experience is an ongoing journey and it is okay not to have all the answers. This profound awareness rewarded me with a sense of freedom that I never knew was possible.

Trusting the mystery brought me peace and gave me the freedom of choice. I welcome the grace of the Holy Spirit and the dualistic nature of my soul. I accept that which I cannot change and now view these situations as challenges and opportunities for growth instead of limitations that keep me from fulfilling my fullest potential. Surrendering to a power greater than my ego empowered me to go forward in a light of soulfulness. Letting go of my resistance to change opened new doors for me, changing my life for the better. Surrendering to my mental confusion put me in touch with my soul; letting go of my confusion gave me back my spirit. For change to occur we must first accept our present reality.

I have asked you to be a witness to your soul and all its emotional manifestations. Feel it, embrace it, do not deny its importance, for resistance only creates more pain and suffering. Then work through and let go of these raw emotions, releasing them. Acceptance means we are going with the natural flow of universal energy, the force of the Divine Spirit. Acceptance is about magic and the mystery. It is positive. Acceptance makes growth and change possible.

155

In this chapter I have suggested some coping strategies that I and others who have found the strength and courage to go forward have realized on our paths toward healing. I encourage you to explore them. Some of these strategies may work for you; others may not. Use your imagination and creative self to peel back the layers of your psychological pain and suffering so that you can heal the heart and soul of your beingness. Healing is a journey of self-discovery as we choose to minister to the emotionality of loss, separation, and grief. It is through this process that we come to a place of celebrating life.

The next chapter explores some theoretical approaches to understanding our emotions and our human reactions to them. The soul is connected to both our unconscious mind and our conscious awareness, which together affect our physiology. This mind-body connection, the material self, interacts with our social self and spiritual self, becoming a more Holistic Self. We can best realize our wholeness, or holy...ness, by bringing balance to the mind, body, soul, and spirit of our human beingness.

> *You would know the secret of death. But how shall you find it unless you seek it in the heart of life? ... For death and life are one, even as the river and the sea are one.*
>
> —Kahlil Gibran

> *Anytime we see the truth and fail to act, we begin to die.*
>
> —M. Joycelyn Elders

11

The Gift of Awareness

> *I believe that our emotions are voices of
> the soul, symbols sculptured in the
> language of the heart, and like Jungian
> archetypes and whispering dreams, they
> are powerful messengers to help us
> balance the energies of our human
> beingness.*
>
> —Helen Elaine

It is important to explore how the human soul interacts with
our biological self, our mental awareness, and our socialized
perceptions, because our emotions are intrinsically interwoven
throughout the Holistic Self and all these components affect
our beliefs, attitudes, and behaviors. This chapter is devoted to
acknowledging the physiological, mental, and social aspects of
human emotionality as it relates to loss and grief. The theoreti-
cal perspectives I discuss in this chapter—biofeedback and
somatics, emotional intelligence, and symbolic interactionism—
were key in my understanding the concept of "healing thyself."

I do not feel that we can heal our soul and spirit independent of
the physical body or that the physical body can be healed indepen-
dent of the mind, soul, and spirit. Each person is a synthesis of all
these components which must be considered in healing the psyche's
sense of separation and anxiety. First, I will discuss the mind-body
connection and then the Soma's relationship to the social self.

Of The Soma

The fact is, the realization of loss and subsequent grief are stressors on the physical human organism. The degree to which an individual assigns meaning or importance to the anxiety and stress of each life situation influences how long that person will carry the stress in his or her body. A loss creates initial distress, and the way we individually handle or do not handle it causes additional stress. It is this secondary stress that does the most damage to the body and the psyche. We owe our recognition of the concept of stress to endocrinologist Hans Selye, who explained that our health and happiness depends on our ability to adjust to all the changes in our environment.

The works of Thomas Hanna and Eleanor Criswell provided me with an understanding of the physiological responses of the mind-body connection. I recommend their books, *Somatics: Reawakening the Mind's Control of Movement, Flexibility, and Health* and *Biofeedback and Somatics* respectively, to all my students as they are both conclusive and easily comprehended. Hanna extends Seyle's biochemical understanding of stress to include the sensory motor aspect. He refers to the neuromuscular adaptation to sustained negative stress ("distress" or the withdrawal response) as the Red Light reflex and sustained positive stress ("eustress" or the action response) as the Green Light reflex.[1]

My body has chronically experienced both these conditions. The Red Light reflex was caused by childhood fear and the traumatic event of my auto accident. These responses to distressing events were learned at the unconscious level or what Hanna would term a "habituation process," meaning slowly over time. The neuromuscular response to enduring the rigors of academia for six years sustained the Green Light reflex within my body. These are normal and automatic reactions of our neuromuscular system to cope with both positive and negative stressors.

Both physical and psychological injuries or traumas to the Soma, which remember means "living body," cause the human organism great pain and suffering. If we lose both our motor control and our sensory awareness of movement, then we experience what Hanna calls *Sensory-Motor Amnesia*[2] , which I still have, but to a lesser degree, as I practice somatic and biofeedback healing techniques. Somatics are not exercises but movements that help us unlock the posttraumatic stress and/or habituated state at the physical level. There are millions of Americans who suffer with back, shoulder, and neck pain as I do. This physical pain causes tremendous emotional grief as we discussed in Chapter Six. Somatic awareness and education has been instrumental in my healing.

Another important component of my healing process has been biofeedback. In her book *Biofeedback and Somatics*, Dr. Criswell says:

> *Biofeedback measures subconscious physiological functions*
> *... Biofeedback (self-regulation) is a natural part of the*
> *body's function. The primary goal of ongoing self-regulation*
> *is homeostasis, the balance an organism must achieve to*
> *sustain life.*[3]

I first encountered biofeedback one year after my auto accident when my neurosurgeon sent me to a psychotherapist for treatment. I had previously learned the benefits of meditation and autohypnosis, so I was a good candidate for biofeedback. The psychotherapist, who treated me for ten sessions, conscientiously and therapeutically ran me through the biofeedback process; it brought little relief due to my lack of understanding of the mind-body connection. It wasn't until I took Dr. Criswell's psychology course that I began to realize the ultimate benefit from this art of healing. Finally, I understood the mind-body connection and how it was intrinsically interrelated to my emotional and spiritual state of well-being. Not everyone has the opportunity to take such a wonderful course, which is why I recommend her book. Biofeedback, with devotion and attention to healing one's self, can become a lifetime practice of experiencing loving the Holistic Self.

In the following quote, Dr. Criswell shares with us how biofeedback works:

> *There are two basic theories as to how biofeedback works ... The two basic theories are behaviorism and information theory. The behavioristic theory of biofeedback rests on the idea that the feedback signal is a reinforcer. The information theory of biofeedback refers to the idea that biofeedback provides the person with information about his or her body's function. With increased information there is a more effective use of the body on many levels.*[4]

160

This information helps us to understand the human body's automatic, physiological responses so that we can mentally make adjustments to alleviate the stress that our body is enduring. This is a psychosomatic-spiritual experience: we must quiet the mind and body to become in tune with what's going on inside of us. As various instrumentation and modalities read and record our physiological status, they serve as guides within a feedback loop to tell us when our body is out of balance. We can then make conscious adjustments to regulate our physiology, which realigns our Holistic Self.

There are various modalities that record changes in our physiology which enable us to recognize what stress does to our body. For example, an electroencephalograph (EEG) is used to feedback brain-wave activity and is useful for people who suffer with migraine headaches, insomnia, epilepsy, and other conditions. Skin temperature feedback (ST) is being used for patients who suffer with hypertension, Raynaud's disease, and asthma. Another useful measurement is electrodermal activity (EDA), which measures the electrical characteristics of the skin and is used to treat people with phobias and anxiety, hypertension, stuttering, and other biological reactions to stress.[5] I use EMG or electromyographic feedback because my major stressors affect the muscles. Using EMG feedback helped me with pain control through an awareness of the tension in my muscles caused by improper movement, overuse, and stress. I have learned how to change my contracted muscles in my shoulders and neck to states of relaxation.

One might ask, "How do we consciously change our physiology?" One of the main tenets of biofeedback is that it is a first-person healing process. Biotechnicians are educators and trainers. They teach the client to "heal thyself." This form of healing becomes a mindful, spiritual practice that we can do for twenty minutes a day in our own home. I am interested in sharing with you how this psychophysiological art of healing correlates with emotional pain and suffering.

As we are threatened by the stimuli in our environment (both physical and/or psychological stress or eustress—pain and suffering), we go into a *flight or fight* response mode. This means our central nervous system (CNS), which consists of our brain and spinal cord (the overall system that controls the body), goes from a parasympathetic nervous system (PNS) dominance to one of increased sympathetic nervous system (SNS) activity. When this occurs and the CNS is continuously aroused, we shift from homeostasis to a state of hyperalertness. Dr. Criswell explains:

> *Characteristic changes of the sympathetic nervous system accompany this process. These changes include increased heart rate; increased blood pressure; increased blood flow to the brain; spinal cord and muscles; decreased gastrointestinal activity; decreased blood clotting time; pupil dilation; and brainwave shift to beta—all parts of the preparation for fighting or running (the fight or flight*

response). Activation of the SNS continues until the factors causing the increased arousal decrease or the person becomes habituated.[6]

In biofeedback training we learn to control or adjust the above-mentioned physiological conditions. Biofeedback is generally experienced in conjunction with relaxation and breathing techniques. As we mindfully experience abdominal or diaphragmatic breathing, relax or drop the jaw, and use our imagination to focus on relaxing our muscles and all parts of our body, we can reverse our hyperactive state of sympathetic nervous system to one of parasympathetic activity or homeostasis. This requires practice but becomes a useful tool in coping with not only the traumatic events of life, but the little everyday stressors as well.

162

I teach my students and clients how to breathe from the abdomen by slowly inhaling through the nose (a four-count) and exhaling from the mouth (a six-count) while gently pushing the stomach out on the inhale and letting it return to its natural, relaxed position on the exhale. Mindful attention to one's breathing begins the quieting process of mind-body, which relaxes the sympathetic nervous system. As we consciously change the rhythms of our breathing, several things begin to occur. To quote Criswell: "The purposes of breathing exercises include psycho-physical relaxation, rejuvenation, the release of dormant energies and the creation of mental serenity."[7]

The classic pose is a reclined position, free from the restraint of tight clothing, and accompanied with progressive relaxation and sense withdrawal. These conditions combine to allow a return of the central nervous system to a parasympathetic dominance or homeostasis. The idea is to check in with your body and relax from head to toe. When you work on a particular area of your body (for example, I often focus on my right trapezius muscle which is contracted from writing), various visualization techniques may be used adjunctively for maximum healing benefit. Personally, I use biofeedback and meditation several times a day. It has dramatically changed my life; it has given me less pain, less stress, the ability to concentrate and focus, and generally a happier personality. I find it to be an avenue for getting in touch with my soul.

I have learned to be *present* in mind, body, and soul, which connects me to the Divine Spirit and my creative spiritual self— my core essence. I highly recommend both somatics and bio-feedback as a road to coping with stress, promoting healing, and finding enlightenment. Because of these ongoing practices, I have learned to *be* with my feelings. The reality of being my Holistic Self enables me to feel my pain and suffering and the suffering of others, without getting stuck in the abyss. These alternative healing practices, being conscious of the Both/And...ness of the human experience, and meditation have re-warded me with the ability to appreciate the mind-body-soul-spirit connection.

163

Mental Awareness of Emotions

Daniel Goleman's book, *Emotional Intelligence*, an inclusive study drawing on groundbreaking brain and behavioral research, un-derscores the reality that emotions are integral to understand-ing human behavior and fulfillment of human potential. I highly recommend this book for everyone. Though it is packed full of research, Goleman brings simplicity and understanding to a complex science. He writes very sensitively about the reality of contemporary psychosocial issues and has much to offer in the study of human emotion. He states:

> *The intuitive signals that guide us in these moments come in the form of limbic-driven surges from the Viscera that Damasio calls "somatic markers"— literally, gut feelings. The somatic marker is a kind of automatic alarm, typically*

*calling attention to a potential danger from a given course
of action....Whenever such a gut feeling rises up, we can
immediately drop or pursue that avenue of consideration
with greater confidence, and so pare down our array of
choices to a mere manageable decision matrix. The key to
sounder personal decision-making, in short: being attuned
to our feelings.*[8]

Understanding that we are beings who have both a think-
ing brain and an emotional brain, we can learn to influence
our emotional responses to bring about a balance within the
Holistic Self.

Within science there is an ongoing debate as to how to clas-
sify emotions. Keeping within the Zeitgeist of the mind-body-
soul-spirit paradigm, I believe that our emotions are voices of
the soul, symbols sculptured in the language of the heart, and
like Jungian archetypes and whispering dreams, they are pow-
erful messengers to help us balance the energies of our human
beingness.

Deepak Chopra, author of *Ageless Body, Timeless Mind*, assumes
that "the biochemistry of the body is a product of awareness.
Beliefs, thoughts, and emotions create the chemical reactions
that uphold life in every cell."[9] As science has evolved, we have
come a long way from merely relying on the right-brain/left-
brain theory of the human mind. We now know that the human
brain is a complex system of circuitry that works as a feedback
loop relaying energy and information to and from all parts of
the human organism.

As this concept relates to the pain and suffering of loss and
separation, I have suggested that the healing process is in part
acknowledging our emotions. Working through our emotions
is not about acting out inappropriately during our grieving/heal-
ing process, as this only creates additional pain and suffering. If
we have not learned to feel our feelings and react appropriately,

what Goleman calls *emotional intelligence*, then we can relearn how to do this. The lifelong process that I refer to as healing, or ministering to the needs of the soul, is our opportunity to develop our emotional intelligence. It is our opportunity for growth and expansion of consciousness—our opportunity to walk in the light of love and compassion.

Of the Social Self

Another way of looking at this complex issue of integrating our emotional and rational selves with our social self is symbolic interactionism, a theory I found to be of great value in my healing process. Symbolic interactionism (SI) is a sociological social-psychology perspective that is rooted in the philosophy of pragmatism, or that which is practical. This approach appeals to me because, although I offer a wide array of ideas and methods when ministering to clients who are enduring pain and suffering, I am a pragmatist at heart. I believe that ideas and concepts are only true if they work. However, I also recognize that what works for one individual does not necessarily work for another.

I have been guided by John P. Hewitt's *Self and Society*, a theoretical view of symbolic interactionism. As we are social beings and our sense of loss and grief are often influenced by social constraints, it is appropriate to consider our social self in our healing. Hewitt's perspective acknowledges that the meaning or purpose we mortals place on our experiences affects us to varying degrees. We give meaning to things by symbols and language, which are interpreted through the functions of our thinking brain. The suggestion that we are self-referential means that we are both an acting subject and a passive object of our experiences. Therefore, we are both what happens to us (the object of an experience) and the subject of our taking action in response to our experiences.[10] When emotions arise unconsciously or consciously in the events of trauma or loss, we can make a choice on how to react. Our human relationships are at the root of much of our loss and grief. We have the potential to form our conduct within our interactions with others through our pain and suffering as well as in our healing process.

Hewitt explains that we, as members of society and culture, are the products of our reactions and behaviors (conduct) as I have mentioned in regards to death, loss, and grief. I believe that as a culture we have neglected to take a serious look at these issues: this avoidance keeps us prisoners of fear. As we reeducate ourselves to the benefits of applying what we can learn through the study of death and grief to our more ordinary losses of living, we can reshape and constrain human conduct to one of more balance and peace.

The SI perspective assumes that we are evolving creatures in a process of change—each person is a self in an ongoing process of being or becoming. We are active, reflective, and interpretive selves, and through experiences our meanings and interpretations or understandings can and do change.[11] The meanings and values we place on our challenges and opportunities are emergent, and it is through our problematic experiences that new or different meanings emerge. Our losses, separations, and processes of detachment are certainly those that qualify as being problematic to the developing psyche. It is when we process these experiences of the heart that we come into new awareness.

If we take the time to reflect on our experience of loss and grief, and all experiences of life, we realize that these experiences inform our meanings and beliefs. This is a time of reexamination. The death of a loved one and other losses are opportunities to reevaluate our attitudes, beliefs, and previously established meanings so that we can change them to balance the splintering of the soul. We cannot take for granted that others' meanings are the same as ours. This is a personal journey of self-discovery. However, I feel it is wise to be aware of how our

166

meanings and interpretations may affect others. This helps us to have understanding and reverence for our choices and those of others, even when the two differ.

Through active, conscious participation in our experiences, we begin to transform ourselves. Taking a risk to step outside our known reality and bravely changing our consciousness rewards us with a higher level of growth. This process in itself may present a sense of loss and grief. It is difficult to let go of old beliefs, attitudes, and meanings; but we can do it and must do it so as to evolve individually and collectively into a humanity of peace and love.

I experienced this when I let go of my socialized ideas of my roles in life. I formed new meanings that more comfortably aligned with my Holistic Self. I used to be a linear black-or-white thinker. I have learned that this is dangerous. When we think only in terms of absolutes, whether negative or positive, we are limited. I felt I was either all good or all bad, all right or all wrong. This is judgmental. Reading the works of Jung, Hillman, Moore, Wilber, Chopra, Houston, and Zukav, I began to realize the Both/And...ness of our human reality. Human beings are not all good or all bad. Our experiences of being "unconditional spirits trapped in conditions" are neither all pain and suffering nor all joyous celebrations. The truth is that the human experience is about both of these, and much, much more.

By reflecting on our experiences we can reevaluate and redefine our *attitudes, beliefs*, and *behaviors*. This is how we change and evolve. We arrive at new *meanings* that enable us to move forward. I believe that with a deeper understanding of the mind-body connection and its correlation to the social self, we can begin to heal the psyche on both an individual and collective level. By integrating theory with personal experience, we rediscover how the soul is delicately interwoven into the essence of human emotion and begin to explore the mystery of our human beingness. I did this by peeling back the layers of the psychological pain and suffering inherent in my losses and ministering to the emotional needs of my grieving soul—revealing my esoteric heart which connects me to you, the spirit of humanity, unity consciousness, and to God.

I pray that disclosing my personal experience and understanding of loss, separation, grief, and anxiety eases some of the pain for those who are suffering. Also, I hope this book will be instrumental in assisting all professionals as we interact with each individual we are blessed to work with. We all have a great deal to learn about love and compassion. Will compassion and love solve humanity's pain and suffering? Maybe—maybe not! But, I can assure you, it will make an enormous impact, and for the better.

168   As I continue to experience daily living, I sometimes still feel that others don't really understand my pain and that my situation is unique and different. All the books, counselors, advice, etc., are helpful. I understand what their message is. But, when I am struggling with the darker side of the soul, my negative emotions, I cannot always muster the strength and energy to practice my new "insights" in the present situation. All this information becomes data and knowledge. How do I keep sane today? How do I live one day at a time? I know all this stuff; it's logical, it makes sense. What is wrong with me that I am depressed and can't walk the walk, do the work it takes to heal?

Have you ever felt this way? After reading *Artichoke Heart*, do you still feel this way? Please do not despair. Everything that you feel, and everything that I feel, is the human experience. We have bright and sunny days; we have dark and fearful days. This is NORMAL. It is part of the soul's journey. Today we do the best we can; tomorrow we will do the best we can. Together we will survive. Awareness gives us the opportunity to grow and change. This is BOTH a conscious AND unconscious process.

Change and transition take time. Be gentle with yourself, following the rhythm that is naturally yours. Let it be okay to have sad days. Likewise, let it be okay to have happy days. Let it be okay to "not get it"—to not have all the answers.

I keep struggling with my physical pain and my emotional scars. I know that facing the darker side of the soul, residing in the abyss of pain and suffering, is what allows us to hold hands with or witness love, peace, and compassion. These are manifestations of the Divine Spirit. It is our journey <u>through</u> the darkness that brings us into the light; we cannot have one without the other. After fifty years of traveling this earthly path I realize that the more I learn, the more I know, the more I experience life…the more I have yet to learn, yet to know, and yet to live. This gives me hope. This keeps me humble and in awe of the mystery. You, too, will find your own path. You will explore and discover what your meaning and purpose is. I believe as we age the knowledge and emotional scar tissue that one gathers over a lifetime turns into wisdom and grace. Please trust yourself. Trust the process of living. Have faith that grieving all our losses is really a process of nurturing and healing the soul.

169

Sometimes being human is going two steps forward and three steps back. Being human is making mistakes, making good and bad choices, being imperfect. Learn from all experience and celebrate *being* in the world. I find it helpful to reevaluate our vocabulary. Instead of saying *survived, recovered,* or *healed,* which indicate a beginning and an end to a process, perhaps we should say *surviving, recovering,* and *healing,* which indicate an ongoing process. Using *ing* words put things into a different and more manageable perspective. Life is hard; living is do…able.

So, take it easy. Learn to love yourself. Learn to like yourself. Have fun, relax, and learn to play. Laugh and cry. Try new things, like some of the suggested coping or healing techniques offered in *Artichoke Heart.* If you can do some of them some days and not other days, let this be okay. Keep this book in a safe place and return to it occasionally; perhaps you will become aware of some new ideas in the second, third, or fourth reading. I always discover something new when I reread a book. Trust your higher power, trust the Spirit within you. Trust your intuition; embrace your suffering. Go with the energy of life. Make a conscious choice to keep trying. As time passes, your emotional pain (grief) will become gentler and easier to manage. Eventually, your sorrows will turn into energy of light and love, and you will be doing what you were put on this earth to do—You Will Be LIVING!

> *The ordinariness of human experience should be a continuing journey of rediscovering soul, and a constant devotion to and celebration of the Divine Spirit.*
>
> —*Helen Elaine*

12

A Season of Transcendence

> Living is a journey of discovery. Dying
> is a process of returning. Let us honor
> the sacredness of death. And, celebrate
> the mystery of Life.
>
> —Helen Elaine

I know *everything* comes full circle. Being raised on a farm, I witnessed the emergence of life with spring planting, the natural stages of growth in the summer, and the decaying process of death as we annually harvested the yearly crops. In the autumn, as the leaves on the trees turned a golden brown, we stripped the fields bare and left the earth vulnerable to winter's sub-zero temperatures and tempest manifestations. This changing of seasons, this ongoing reality of energy exchange, goes on cyclically, unnoticed by many and appreciated by only a few. I am blessed to have been raised in an environment of such profound beauty and wonderment.

The solar systems, the planets, the stars, and everything in the heavens are on a magical and mysterious journey. On the planet earth, we mortals are an intricate part of this great tapestry of *life*, as all of Creation is the very breath of God. The soul is our connection to the Spirit of all that is. As we all work together to cultivate the mind of human potential, minister to the emotional and psychological needs of those who suffer, and tend to the heart of humanity, this will surely become a more peaceful, loving, and joyous journey for us all. The human spirit is resilient, and we have rediscovered that our soul is present to assist us with the seasons of change.

A Truck Full of Angels

A year and a half ago I had a profound and sacred experience. This glimpse into the mystery of life was as powerful as when I gave birth to both of my beautiful daughters. However, this passage was just the opposite of bringing life into *this* world. I had the privilege of being by my brother-in-law's side as he prepared for his transcendence to the *other* world. Phil, who was only fifty-two years old, was in the last stages of cancer, an eighteen-month journey which he lived through without complaint, and with the grace and dignity of a saint.

172 Hospice colleagues had shared with me this privilege of witnessing their client's preparation to leave this world; but, because I did bereavement counseling instead of being a caretaker, I had never been with anyone when they died. During Phil's long illness, I offered to go to Iowa and be with my sister and her husband during his last weeks. When my sister telephoned, I was on the next plane.

Autumn in the Midwest is so beautiful. The trees were shimmering with red, orange, and gold leaves with hints of green still peeking through. The rolling hills seemed to go on forever. It was October and the air was crisp and clean. As my nephew drove me from the Omaha airport to the little town in Iowa where I was born and raised, I sensed a silence and stillness that I had never before experienced on my many trips home. Yes, a part of me still considers Iowa my home. This trip seemed different and I didn't know why. I remember asking God for guidance as to how to help Marcy and Phil through this sacred, yet troubling time.

When I arrived I felt the same mysterious silence and calmness in their home, which looked very much like a hospital to accommodate Phil's needs. Phil had requested that he die at home. I felt such an overwhelming sense of peace that I didn't understand, as I assumed this would be a very unsettling experience. It was not. I will not discuss the angelic care that Marcy performed accept to say two things: (1) I do not know how she kept going, she was still working at the dental office in the daytime and tending to Phil around the clock, and (2) she never complained or gave up hope. I was in awe of her strength, courage, faith, and devotion to her husband. I was honored that I could give her some much-needed respite. My other sisters, my nieces and nephews, and friends had been helping all these months and continued to offer support and love. On the days Phil could, he had visitors. As the weeks passed, we had to limit visits to family only, a few at a time.

As I held Phil's hand by day and prayed through the night, I learned many things.

173

Some things are to sacred to share with others; however, I will try to convey some of my lingering memories which might help others appreciate the mystery of transcendence. It seemed like when Phil and I were alone, the grace of his transformation was filtering into every cell of my body. This is hard to explain, but I felt an ongoing osmosis between the two of us, resulting in a metamorphosis for me. Gifts of awareness, gratitude, and humility were filling my heart with an abundance of love. I was aware that he and I were in the very close presence of God. I realized I was blessed to be part of such a large family. Since my mother's death, Marcy and Phil had become the matriarch and patriarch of the clan, roles that were difficult at times and entangled with much sadness. I thanked Phil for his love, devotion, and constant support of our family with all its dysfunction.

Every morning before the rituals of caring for Phil began, I had my coffee and cigarettes followed by twenty minutes of meditation on their sun porch. This had been Phil's favorite room in their home and I am sure he was missing its comfort. The quiet of early mornings, the squirrels running along the utility wires and leaping onto tree branches, the gorgeous sunrises, the distant whistles and clanking noises of trains as they moved through town on iron rails, these are the sights and sounds that nurtured my soul. I smiled to myself one morning as I recalled one of the last bits of dialogue in Kevin Costner's movie *A Field Of Dreams*: "Is this Heaven?" "No, it's Iowa."

The peace and serenity I felt the day when the first snow-flakes of the season swirled from the sky and blanketed our little town was metaphorically for me a renewal of life. Everything was so pure and clean. Amidst all this spiritual nourishment, I became aware of the polarities of my soul. I experienced a daily reality of fighting back my tears of sadness and my deep concern for my sister's personal hell of loss and grief, while at the same time, feeling a sense of acceptance, joy, and peace for my brother as he was preparing to rejoin God. I remember feeling like I was floating through this experience as if time, the weeks, hours, and minutes had no meaning. It was a reality outside of time-bound awareness—it was just *being*. I know we were experiencing unity consciousness.

Because I had moved to the West Coast some thirty years earlier, Phil and I had not been close friends. Memories flooded my mind about our double-dating in high school, he and Marcy, my husband and I. We were all good friends back then and went through a lot together due to my father's alcoholism. I remembered all the horrors as well as all the laughs the four of us shared, both couples' wedding days, and how much we all meant to one another, still mean to one another. The love present in their home brought back memories of my love for my husband and our children and all the blessed years we had together as a family. These memories helped me to put my marriage and divorce in a different perspective, a place of renewed acceptance and appreciation for both. I also began to see my parents in a new light, knowing they did the best they

174

could, Dad with his disease of alcoholism and Mom raising nine children as a battered woman.

Watching Phil live with such dignity through his process of transcendence and witnessing Marcy's ongoing devotion to and faith in God taught me a great deal about love, compassion, and the meaning of life. I finally knew the reason for the peace, calmness, and serenity that enveloped my environment. It was about love. Marcy's love for Phil and her love of God, Phil's love for Marcy and his love of God, and God's love for them BOTH. Their home was so full of God's presence that I was an automatic recipient of the this abundance of overflowing energy—this form of energy being all that is really important in this world—the energy of *love*. I felt truly blessed and will be forever grateful.

One day Phil was trying to get out of bed. He often tried to do this but could not as he was paralyzed from the waist down due to the cancer in his spine. Holding his hand and stroking his arm, I asked him where he wanted to go. He said, "Get my shoes and pants. I need to go out back." Once again, I explained to him that his legs did not work, and instead of tears rolling down his face which is what usually happened when he wanted to go somewhere and couldn't, he continued to speak in a weak but determined voice. He said, "Don't you hear the music?" I said, "No, but let me listen closer…oh yes, now I hear it." Of course, I did not hear it but I knew he did. Shivers began to ease through my body like a warm summer breeze. "There is a truck in the backyard and they are waiting for me. Don't you hear them singing and dancing to the music?" And so, I asked, "Who is waiting for you?" Then that wonderful crooked smile appeared on his face, the one Phil always wore when he was aware of something that no one else knew, like a little boy who knew he was getting a puppy for Christmas. He replied, "The angels, they want me to go with them." After taking a slow deep breath I reassured him that I, too, had heard someone earlier in the back yard and I now realized who they were and why they had come. Rubbing his head, gen-

175

tly touching his face, and holding his hand, I explained to Phil that everything was all right. The angels would wait for him and when he was ready, he should go with them. He settled down and before he went to sleep, I told him how much we loved him and that we would take care of Marcy for him.

The following week Phil was having difficulty breathing, could hardly eat or drink, and Marcy began sleeping on a makeshift cot by his hospital bed. She and I talked very little as I knew she must be allowed to go through this process her way. This was a special and sacred time for them. On the evening of November 18th, the energy began to shift in the house and I knew I must not go to bed. The silence cannot be put into words. I sat up praying on my rosary beads while they held hands and slept peacefully. I was only a few feet away. At four my head and neck were aching, so I decided to go to my room and rest, knowing I would be of no use to them in the morning if I did not get some sleep. At four-thirty Marcy woke me and said, "Helen, I think Phil's gone." I ran to the living room, paused, then leaned down and kissed Phil good-bye. I knew the truck full of angels had taken him home.

Through the pain and suffering which we have shared, and continue to share, my sisters and I have become much closer than we have been in years. What a wonderful gift! I now realize that all the sense of unfairness in life is really about learning, growing, and giving and receiving love. It seems so simple yet in this physical world it becomes so complicated.

Since my experience with Phil and Marcy, I realize how fortunate I am. Though I have very little income, I am a wealthy woman, filled with the richness of love from my daughers, sisters, dear friends, and Mort. I can only try to live with my disability in the spirit of courage and dignity shown to me by my sister and her husband.

Living in the conscious presence of my soul will keep my heart open to the truth, keep me balanced through the spiraling emotional events of life's challenges, and at the same time, keep me humble and appreciative of all life's blessings. The human experience is definitely about the Both/And...ness of being a *spiritual being* residing in a physical world of matter.

Because emotion, music, and poetry are expressions, voices of the soul, I find it appropriate to conclude my dialogue with you in verse.

The Mystery

Knowing we are souls manifest in physical form,
rejoice in the wisdom that the human experience
is a wonderful gift from the Creator.   177

Life is a beautiful journey,
inclusive of **Both** sadness and joy.
The polarities of the soul balance the dichotomy
of being both spiritual and physical beings.

The soul is a descendant of unity consciousness,
and is **Both** light and darkness.
The soul is our connection to the Divine Spirit, to **God**.
The Spirit is our connection to each other, our **One...ness**.

Living is a journey of discovery.
Dying is a process of returning.
Let us honor the sacredness of death.
And, celebrate the mystery of life.

This paradox—the mystery—is full of questions and doubt.
We'll never have all the answers; the quest is our birthright.

Balancing the rhythms of the dance;
escorted by choirs of angels.
We suffer through our **losses**; rejoicing in all our **blessings**.

With reopened hearts and a raised consciousness,
we begin to understand the profound musical message:
"I could have missed the pain,
but I would have had to miss the **dance**."[1]

As we walk upon this planet, we are in charge of each other.
Let us not fall short of reverence, gratitude, and responsibility.
Everything we are, think, say, and do affects **all** of Creation.
Love thyself, and love thy **neighbor**.

178   And so my Dear Friends,
gather around unto thy selves and to each other;
singing and dancing the music of life.
Celebrating both our one…ness and our individual uniqueness.

We can honor being of **Both** worlds;
the sacred and the profane, the spiritual and the physical.
God, beauty, and love are all around us:
below us, above us, and in us.

Yes, in **US**! Each and Every One of Us.

Notes

1: *Recognizing the Emotional Soul*

1 Thomas Moore, *Care of the Soul: A Guide For Cultivating Depth And Sacredness In Everyday Life* (New York: HarperPerennial, 1992). I am grateful to Thomas Moore for offering us new vocabulary, that is both soft and poignant, in response to the needs of the soul. I use his terms *caring for, tending to, ministering to,* and *cultivating* as I teach, counsel, and write.

2 Kahlil Gibran, *The Prophet* (New York: Alfred A. Knopf, 1926), 51.

3 William James, *Psychology: Briefer Course* (New York: Henry Holt, 1907).

4 Jean Houston, *The Search for The Beloved: Journeys in Mythology and Sacred Psychology* (Mill Valley, CA: J. P. Tarcher, 1987). I am indebted to Jean for her wonderful sense of the grandness of the spirit. I often use her *much, much more* expression and her awareness of the *Both/And...ness* of this human journey.

5 Thomas Moore, *Care of the Soul.*

6 Jean Houston, *The Search for The Beloved.* Thanking her again for her spiritual understanding of God.

2: Memories and the Mystery

1   Harvey Mindess, *Makers of Psychology: The Personal Factor* (New York: Insight Books, 1988), 15.

2   Elie Wiesel, *Night* (New York: Bantam, 1982), ix.

3   Deepak Chopra, *Ageless Body, Timeless Mind: The Quantum Alternative to Growing Old* (New York: Harmony Books, 1993), 298.

4   M. Scott Peck, *Further Along the Road Less Traveled: The Unending Journey Towards Spiritual Growth* (New York: Simon & Schuster, 1993) 138.

5   John Bradshaw, *Homecoming: Reclaiming and Championing Your Inner Child* (New York: Bantam, 1990).

6   Ken Wilber, *Grace and Grit: Spirituality and Healing in the Life and Death of Treya Killam Wilber* (Boston: Shambhala, 1993).

7   Thomas Moore, *Care Of The Soul.*

3: The Paradox of Life and Death

1   Ernest Becker, *The Denial of Death* (New York: Free Press, 1973), 69.

2   Calvin Hall and Gardner Linzey, *Theories of Personality* (New York: John Wiley & Sons, 1978), 37-39.

3   Ibid., 38.

4   Ibid., 32.

5   From Paul Tillich, "The Eternal Now" edited by Herman Feifel in *The Meaning of Death* (New York: McGraw, 1965), 9.

6   Ken Wilber, *Grace and Grit*, 82.

7   Thomas Moore, *Care of the Soul*.

8   Ibid., 296-297.

9   Paul Tillich, "The Eternal Now" edited by Herman Feifel in *The Meaning of Death*, 32.

4: Discovering the Grief Process

1   Sogyal Rinpoche, *The Tibetan Book of Living and Dying* edited by Patrick Gafney and Andrew Harvey (San Francisco: HarperSanFrancisco, 1994), 311-312.

2   Ibid., 39.

3   Elisabeth Kubler-Ross, *On Death and Dying* (New York: Macmillan, 1976).

4   Judy Tatelbaum, *The Courage to Grieve: Creative Living, Recovery, & Growth Through Grief* (New York: Harper & Row, 1980), 73.

5   David Dietrich and Peter Shabad, *The Problem of Loss and Mourning: A Psychoanalytical Perspective* (Madison, CT, International University Press, 1990).

6   *Webster's New World Thesaurus* edited by Funk & Wagnall (New York: Simon & Schuster, 1993), 328.

7   Sogyal Rinpoche, *The Tibetan Book of Living and Dying*, 29.

5: Development of the Holistic Self

1   Benjamin Lahey, *Psychology: An Introduction* (Boston: McGraw-Hill, 1998), Chapter Eight.

2   Daniel Goleman, *Emotional Intelligence* (New York: Bantam, 1995).

3   Robert Crooks and Jean Stein, *Psychology: Science, Behavior, and Life* (Orlando, FL: Holt, Rinehart & Winston, 1991), 428.

4   Christina and Stanislav Grof, *Spiritual Emergency* (Mill Valley, CA: J. P. Tarcher, 1989).

6: Loving Relationships

1   Thomas Moore, *Care of the Soul*, 14.

2   Harriet Goldhor Lerner, *The Dance of Intimacy: A Woman's Guide to Courageous Acts of Change in Key Relationships* (New York: Harper & Row, 1990).

3   David Dietrich and Peter Shabad, *The Problem of Loss and Mourning*.

4   Ibid.

5   Ibid., 106-107.

6   Ken Wilber, *Grace and Grit*, 209.

7   Harriet Lerner, *The Dance of Intimacy*.

8   John Bradshaw, *Creating Love: The Next Great Stage of Growth* (New York: Bantam, 1992).

9   Ibid., 132.

182

7: All God's Children

1   Rumi, the ancient Sufi, quoted by Deepak Chopra, *Mind, Body, Soul: The Mystery and the Magic* (Atlanta: PBS Special, Turner Home Entertainment).

2   Lorna Catford and Michael Ray, *The Path of the Everyday Hero: Drawing on the Power of Myth to Meet Life's Most Important Challenges* (Los Angeles: J. P. Tarcher, 1991).

3   M. Scott Peck, *Further Along the Road Less Traveled*.

4   David Dietrich and Peter Shabad, *The Problem of Loss and Mourning*, 67-68.

5   Stephen Levine, "The Nature of Healing," in *Thinking Allowed: Conversations on the Leading Edge of Knowledge With Jeffrey Mishlove, Ph.D.* (Tulsa, OK: Council Oak Books, 1992), 352-353.

6   Ken Wilber, *Grace and Grit*, 318.

7   Arthur S. Reber, *The Penguin Dictionary of Psychology* (New York: Penguin Books, 1985), 434.

8   Ronald J. Comer, *Abnormal Psychology* (New York: W. H. Freeman & Company, 1992), 1.

9   M. Scott Peck, *Further Along the Road Less Traveled*, 58-59.   183

10 Ronald T. Potter-Efron and Patricia S. Potter-Efron, *Anger, Alcoholism, and Addictions: Treating Individuals, Couples, and Families* (New York: W. W. Norton & Company, 1991), 8.

11 Helen Elaine, (1995) unpublished graduate research *Applied Psychology of Loss and Grief: The Physiological, Psychosocial, and Spiritual Manifestations of Separation and Anxiety* (Sonoma State University: Rohnert Park, CA).

12 Jody Messler Davies and Mary Gail Frawley, *Treating the Adult Survivor of Childhood Sexual Abuse: A Psychoanalytical Perspective* (New York: Basic Books, 1994), 35.

13 Ibid., 18.

14 Barbara Hamilton, *The Hidden Legacy: Confronting and Healing Three Generations of Incest* (Fort Bragg, CA: Cypress House, 1992), 16.

15 M. E. Ziolko, "Counseling Parents of Children with Disabilities: A Review of the Literature and Implications For Practice," edited in *Perspectives on Disability* by M. Nagler (Palo Alto, CA: Health Market Research, 1993), 185-193.

8: Other Living Losses

1 Janice Harris-Lord, *No Time for Goodbyes* (Ventura, CA: Pathfinder, 1991), 30.

2 Marianne Williamson, (1995) CNN "Larry King Live Special: Miracles and the Extraordinary."

3 Harold S. Kushner, *When Bad Things Happen To Good People* (New York: Avon, 1981), 55.

184 ## 9: Grieving Is Healing

1 Deepak Chopra, *Ageless Body, Timeless Mind*, 34.

2 Ram Dass, "Compassion in Action" in *Thinking Allowed: Conversations on the Leading Edge of Knowledge with Jeffrey Mishlove, Ph.D.*, 326-327.

3 Danah Zohar, *The Quantum Self: Human Nature and Consciousness Defined by the New Physics* (New York: William Morrow & Company, Inc., 1990), 73.

4 Joseph Campbell, "Understanding Mythology" in *Thinking Allowed: Conversations on the Leading Edge of Knowledge with Jeffrey Mishlove, Ph.D.*, 91.

5 Daniel Goleman, *Emotional Intelligence*.

6 Christopher Reeve interview with Barbara Walters, ABC's 20/20, 1996.

7 Daniel Goleman, *Emotional Intelligence*.

10: *From Darkness To Light*

1   Thomas Moore, *Care of the Soul*, 10.

2   Thomas Moore, *Care of the Soul*.

3   Carl G. Jung, *Man and His Symbols* (New York: Anchor, 1964).

4   Lorna Catford and Michael Ray, *The Path of the Everyday Hero*.

5   Sant Rajinder Singh, "Inversion" in *A Parliament of Souls: In Search of Global Spirituality* edited by Michael Tobias, Jane Morrison, and Bittina Gray, (San Fransisco: KQED Books, 1995), 253.

6   Joan Wester Anderson, *Where Angels Walk* (New York: Ballantine Books, 1992), 28.

7   Judy Tatelbaum, *The Courage to Grieve*.

8   Judith Viorst, *Necessary Losses: The Loves, Illusions, Dependencies, and Impossible Expectations That All of Us Have to Give Up in Order to Grow* (New York: Fawcett Gold Medal, 1993).

11: *The Gift of Awareness*

1   Thomas Hanna, *Somatics:Reawakening the Mind's Control of Movement, Flexibility, and Health* (Reading, MASS: Addison-Wesley Publishing, 1990), 45.

2   Thomas Hanna, *Somatics: Reawakening the Mind's Control of Movement, Flexibility, and Health*.

3   Eleanor Criswell Hanna, *Biofeedback and Somatics* (Novato, CA: Freeperson Press, 1987), 20.

4   Ibid., ii.

5   Eleanor Criswell Hanna, *Biofeedback and Somatics.*

6   Ibid., 27.

7   Ibid., 69.

8   Daniel Goleman, *Emotional Intelligence*, 53-54.

9   Deepak Chopra, *Ageless Body, Timeless Mind*, 6.

10 John P. Hewitt, *Self & Society: A Symbolic Interactionist Social Psychology* (Boston: Allyn & Bacon, 1991), 23-28.

11 Ibid.

12: A Season of Transcendence

1   From the Garth Brooks song *The Dance*, written by Tony Arata, produced by Allen Reynolds, Liberty Records, 1991.

Selected Reading

The following books are listed as they complement my work and are most helpful to all who are going through various kinds of transition. Arranged according to subject, I hope you will find them as enlightening as I do. I highly recommend them. Also, these resources are in the bibliography if you need further information on them.

Death and Dying

On Death and Dying by Elisabeth Kubler-Ross.
The Courage to Grieve by Judy Tatelbaum.
Grace and Grit by Ken Wilber.
The Tibetan Book of Living and Dying by Sogyal Rinpoche.
Necessary Losses by Judith Viorst.
The Grief Recovery Handbook by John W. James and Frank Cherry.
Life After Loss: A Personal Guide Dealing with Death, Divorce, Job Change and Relocation by Bob Deits.
Tuesdays With Morrie by Mitch Albom.
Talking About Death: A Dialogue between Parent and Child by Earl A. Grollman.
The Fall of Freddie the Leaf by Leo Buscaglia, Ph. D.
The Problem of Loss and Mourning by David Dietrich and Peter Shabad.
The Psychology of Death by Robert Kastenbaum.
The Meaning of Death edited by Herman Feifel.

Soul and Spirituality

The Path of the Everyday Hero by Lorna Catford and Michael Ray.

The Search for The Beloved by Jean Houston.

Embraced By The Light by Betty J. Eadie.

Crossing the Threshold of Hope by His Holiness John Paul II.

Man and His Symbols Carl G. Jung.

Thinking Allowed:Conversations on the Leading Edge of Knowledge with Jeffrey Mishlove by Jeffrey Mishlove.

Life After Life by Raymond Moody.

Care of the Soul by Thomas Moore.

Soul Mates by Thomas Moore.

Further Along the Road Less Traveled by M. Scott Peck.

Love, Medicine, and Miracles by Bernie Siegal.

Boundaries of the Soul by June Singer.

188   *The World's Religions* by Houston Smith.

A Parliament of Souls by Michael Tobias, Jane Morrison, and Bettina Gray.

No Boundary: Eastern and Western Approaches to Personal Growth by Ken Wilber.

The Seat of the Soul by Gary Zukav.

Celestine Prophecy by James Redfield.

The Soul's Code: In Search Of Character And Calling by James Hillman.

Physics and the Soma

Ageless Body, Timeless Mind by Deepak Chopra.

How Yoga Works by Eleanor Criswell.

Biofeedback and Somatics by Eleanor Criswell Hanna.

Somatics by Thomas Hanna.

Emotional Intelligence by Daniel Goleman.

The Quantum Self by Danah Zohar.

Specialized Psychology

Stigma: Notes on the Management of Spoiled Identity by Erving Goffman.
PTSD/Borderlines in Therapy by Jerome Kroll.
Sidney M. Jourard: Selected Writings edited by Michael Lowman and
    Antoinette and Marty Jourard.
Treating the Adult Survivor of Childhood Sexual Abuse by Jody Messler
    Davis and Gail Frawley.
Anger, Alcoholism, and Addiction by Ronald & Patricia Potter-Efron.
Creating Love by John Bradshaw.
Homecoming by John Bradshaw.

Sociological Perspectives

The Managed Heart by Arlie Russell Hochschild.
The Dance of Intimacy by Harriet Goldhor Lerner.   189
Self and Society by John P. Hewitt.
Research Agendas in the Sociology of Emotions by Theodore D. Kemper.

Bibliography

I have used the following resources in my research for direct quotes and understanding, as well as personal growth and development concerning the wisdom of the heart and soul.

Albom, Mitch. *Tuesdays with Morrie: An Old Man, a Young Man, and Life's Greatest Lesson*. New York: Doubleday, 1997.

Anderson, Joan Wester. *Where Angels Walk*. New York: Ballantine Books, 1992.

Becker, Ernest. *The Denial of Death*. New York: Free Press, 1973.

Bradshaw, John. *Creating Love: The Next Great Stage of Growth*. New York: Bantam, 1992.

Bradshaw, John. *Healing the Shame that Binds You*. Deerfield Beach, FL: Health Communications, 1988.

Bradshaw, John. *Homecoming: Reclaiming and Championing Your Inner Child*. New York: Bantam, 1990.

Buscaglia, Leo. *The Fall of Freddie the Leaf: A Story of Life For All Ages*. New York: Henry Holt & Company, 1982.

Campbell, Joseph. *A Hero with a Thousand Faces*. Princeton, NJ: Princeton University Press, 1973.

Catford, Lorna and Michael Ray. *The Path of the Everyday Hero: Drawing on the Power of Myth to Meet Life's Most Important Challenges*. Los Angeles: J. P. Tarcher, 1991.

Chopra, Deepak. *Ageless Body, Timeless Mind: The Quantum Alternative to Growing Old.* New York: Harmony Books, 1993.

Chopra, Deepak. *Mind, Body, Soul: The Mystery and the Magic.* Atlanta, GA: Public Broadcasting Service, Turner home Entertainment.

Comer, Ronald, J. *Abnormal Psychology.* New York: W. H. Freeman, 1992.

Criswell, Hanna Eleanor. *Biofeedback and Somatics.* Novato, CA: Freeperson Press, 1993.

Criswell, Eleanor. *How Yoga Works: An Introduction to Somatic Yoga.* Novato, CA: Freeperson Press, 1987.

Crooks, R. L. and J. Stein. *Psychology: Science, Behavior, and Life.* Orlando, FL: Holt, Rinehart & Winston, 1991.

Davis, Jody Messler and Mary Gail Frawley. *Treating the Adult Survivor of Childhood Sexual Abuse: A Psychoanalytical Perspective.* New York: Basic Books, 1994.

David Dietrich and Peter Shabad. *The Problem with Loss and Mourning.* Madison. CT: International University Press, 1990.

Deits, Bob. *Life After Loss: A Personal Guide Dealing with Death, Divorce, Job Change and Relocation.* Tucson, AZ: Fisher Books, 1988.

Erikson, Erik H. *Childhood and Society.* New York: Norton, 1963.

Freud, Sigmund. *Creative Writing and Daydreaming,* (Vol. 9, pp.143-153). London: Hogarth, 1908.

Fromm, Eric. *Man For Himself: An Inquiry into the Psychology of Ethics.* New York: Henry Holt, 1947.

Funk & Wagnall. *Webster's New World Thesaurus.* New York: Simon & Schuster, 1993.

Gibran, Kahlil. *The Prophet*. New York: Alfred A. Knopf, 1989.

Goffman, Erving. *Stigma: Notes on the Management of Spoiled Identity*. Englewood Cliffs, NJ: Prentice Hall, 1963.

Goleman, Daniel. *Emotional Intelligence*. New York: Bantam, 1995.

Grof, Christina and Stanislav. *Spiritual Emergency*. Mill Valley, CA: J. P. Tarcher, 1989.

Grollman, Earl A. *Talking About Death: A Dialogue between Parent and Child*. Boston: Beacon Press, 1990.

Hall, C. S. and G. Lindzey. *Theories of Personality*. New York: John Wiley & Sons, 1978.

Hamilton, Barbara. *The Hidden Legacy: Confronting and Healing Three Generations of Incest*. Fort Bragg, CA: Cypress House, 1992.

Hanna, Thomas. *Somatics: Reawakening the Mind's Control of Movement, Flexibility, and Health*. Reading, MA: Addison-Wesley, 1990.

Hewitt, John P. *Self and Society: A Symbolic Interactionist Social Psychology*. Boston: Allyn & Bacon, 1991.

Hillman, James. *The Soul's Code: In Search of Character and Calling*. New York: Warner Books, 1996.

Houston, Jean. *The Search for The Beloved: Journeys in Sacred Psychology*. Mill Valley, CA: J. P. Tarcher, 1987.

James, John W. and Frank Cherry. *The Grief Recovery Handbook: A Step-by-Step Program for Moving Beyond Loss*. New York: HarperPerennial, 1988.

James, William. *Psychology: The Briefer Course*. New York: Henry Holt, 1907.

Jung, Carl G. *Man and His Symbols*. New York: Anchor, 1964.

Kastenbaum, Robert. *The Psychology of Death*. New York: Springer, 1992.

Kemper, Theodore. *Research Agendas in the Sociology of Emotions.* New York: State University Press, 1990.

Kroll, Jerome. *PTSD/Borderline in Therapy: Finding the Balance.* New York: W. W. Norton, 1993.

Kubler-Ross, Elisabeth. *On Death and Dying.* New York: Macmillan, 1976.

Kushner, Harold S. *When Bad Things Happen To Good People.* New York: Avon, 1981.

Lerner, Harriet Goldhor. *The Dance of Intimacy: A Woman's Guide to Courageous Acts of Change in Key Relationships.* New York: Perennial Library, 1990.

Lord, Janice Harris. *No Time for Goodbyes.* Ventura, CA: Pathfinder, 1991.

Maslow, Abraham. *Motivation and Personality.* New York: Harper, 1954.   193

Maslow, Abraham. *Religions, Values, and Peak Experiences.* New York: Harper, 1976.

May, Rollo. *The Discovery of Being.* New York: Norton Books, 1983.

Mindess, Harvey. *Makers of Psychology: The Personal Factor.* New York: Insight Books, 1988.

Mishlove, Jeffrey. *Thinking Allowed: Conversations on the Leading Edge of Knowledge with Jeffrey Mishlove.* Tulsa, OK: Council Oak Books, 1992.

Moore, Thomas. *Care of the Soul: A Guide for Cultivating Depth and Sacredness in Everyday Life.* New York: HarperPerennial, 1992.

Moore, Thomas. *Soul Mates: Honoring the Mysteries of Love and Relationship.* New York: HarperPerennial, 1994.

Peck, M. Scott. *Further Along the Road Less Traveled: The Unending Journey Toward Spiritual Growth.* New York: Simon & Schuster, 1993.

Potter-Efron, Ronald and Patricia. *Anger, Alcoholism, and Addictions: Treating Individuals, Couples, and Families.* New York: W. W. Norton, 1991.

Reber, A.S. *The Penquin Dictionary of Psychology.* New York: Penquin Books, 1985.

Rinpoche, Soygal. *The Tibetan Book of Living and Dying,* edited by P. Gaffney and A. Harvey. San Francisco: Harper, 1994.

Rogers, Carl. *A Way of Being.* Boston: Houghton Mifflin, 1980.

Singer, June. *Boundaries of the Soul:The Perspective of Jung's Psychology.* Tulsa, OK: Council Oak Books, 1992.

Smith, Houston. *The World's Religions: Our Great Wisdom Traditions.* San Francisco: Harper Collins, 1991.

Tatelbaum, Judy. *The Courage to Grieve: Creative Living, Recovery, & Growth Through Grief.* New York: Perennial Library, 1980.

Tavris, Carol. *Anger: The Misunderstood Emotion.* New York: Touchstone, 1989.

Vernant, J. P. *The Origins of Greek Thought.* New York: Cornell University Press, 1989.

Viorst, Judith. *Necessary Losses: The Loves, Illusions, Dependencies, and Impossible Expectations That All of Us Have to Give Up in Order to Grow.* New York: Fawcett Gold Medal, 1993.

Wertheimer, Max. *A Brief History of Psychology.* Fort Worth, TX: Holt, Rinehart, and Winston, 1987.

Wiesel, Elie. *Night.* New York: Bantam, 1989.

Wilber, Ken. *Grace and Grit: Spirituality and Healing in the Life and Death of Treya Killam Wilber.* Boston: Shambhala, 1993.

Wilber, Ken. *No Boundaries: Eastern and Westren Approaches to Personal Growth.* Boston: Shambhala, 1985.

Ziolko, M. E. "Counseling Parents of Children with Disibilities: A Review of the Literature and Implications for Practice" in M. Nagler's *Perspectives on Disibility*. Palo Alto, CA: Health Markets Research, 1993.

Zohar, Danah. *The Quantum Self: Human Nature and Consciousness Defined by the New Physics*. New York: William Morrow and Company, 1990.

Zukav, Gary. *The Seat of the Soul*. New York: Fireside, 1990.

197

Order Form

Qty.	Title	Price	Total
	Artichoke Heart	$14.95	
	Shipping and handling Add $3.50 for orders under $20, add $4.00 for orders over $20		
	Sales tax (WA residents only, add 8.6%.)		
	Total enclosed		

Telephone orders:
Call 1-800-461-1931
Have your Visa or
Mastercard ready.

E–Mail orders:
E–mail your order request
to harapub@foxinternet.net

INTL Telephone orders:
Toll free 1-877-250-5500
Have your credit card
ready.

Fax orders:
Fax completed order form
to (425) 398-1380.

Payment: Please check one
❏ Check
❏ Visa
❏ MasterCard

Postal orders:
Send completed order
form to:
Hara Publishing
P.O. Box 19732
Seattle, WA 98109.

Name on Card: _____

Card #: _____

Expiration Date: _____

Name _____

Address _____

City _____ State _____ Zip _____

Daytime Phone (_____) _____

Quantity discounts are available. Call (425) 398-2780 for more information.

Thank you for your order!